YOUTH SPORTS ARE KILLING ME

SLOWLY...

CODY SEEVERS

Mechanicsburg, PA USA

Published by Sunbury Press, Inc.
Mechanicsburg, Pennsylvania

www.sunburypress.com

Copyright © 2025 by Cody Seevers.
Cover Copyright © 2025 by Sunbury Press, Inc.

Sunbury Press supports copyright. Copyright fuels creativity, encourages diverse voices, promotes free speech, and creates a vibrant culture. Thank you for buying an authorized edition of this book and for complying with copyright laws by not reproducing, scanning, or distributing any part of it in any form without permission. You are supporting writers and allowing Sunbury Press to continue to publish books for every reader. For information contact Sunbury Press, Inc., Subsidiary Rights Dept., PO Box 548, Boiling Springs, PA 17007 USA or legal@sunburypress.com.

For information about special discounts for bulk purchases, please contact Sunbury Press Orders Dept. at (855) 338-8359 or orders@sunburypress.com.

To request one of our authors for speaking engagements or book signings, please contact Sunbury Press Publicity Dept. at publicity@sunburypress.com.

FIRST SUNBURY PRESS EDITION: August 2025

Set in Adobe Garamond | Interior design by Crystal Devine | Cover by Victoria Mitchell | Edited by Lawrence Knorr.

Publisher's Cataloging-in-Publication Data
Names: Seevers, Cody, author.
Title: Youth sports are killing me slowly / Cody Seevers.
Description: First trade paperback edition. | Mechanicsburg, PA : Sunbury Press, 2025.
Summary: Navigating youth sports has become a full-time job for parents, driven by dreams of their child reaching the "big stage." But are we doing this for the right reasons, or is the $480 billion sports industry exploiting us? We must refocus on the true purpose of sports—teamwork, resilience, and growth—teaching values that shape success in life, not just in athletics.
Identifiers: ISBN : 979-8-88819-315-0 (paperback).
Subjects: SPORTS & RECREATION / General | SELF-HELP / Motivational & Inspirational | EDUCATION / Leadership.

Designed in the USA
0 1 1 2 3 5 8 13 21 34 55

For the Love of Books!

To Aislynn and Ezra—

You are my greatest joy, my proudest achievement, and my constant inspiration. Watching you grow, compete, and chase your dreams has been one of the greatest privileges of my life.

I hope that through sports, you've learned not just how to win and lose, but how to lead, persevere, and rise above challenges. No matter where life takes you, know that your worth is never measured by a scoreboard, but by the kindness, strength, and character you carry with you.

I will always be your biggest fan.

With all my love,

Dad

CONTENTS

Acknowledgments   vii
Prologue   ix
Introduction   1

CHAPTERS

One.	Where It All Started	3
Two.	The Passion	11
Three.	Parents Are Running Youth Sports	16
Four.	Heading to the MLB	19
Five.	Coaches Are Not Perfect	34
Six.	Referees Don't Get Paid Enough	38
Seven.	Managing the Stress as a Parent	40
Eight.	Always Follow the Coach, Not the Organization	52
Nine.	Your Marriage	59
Ten.	Baseball	68
Eleven.	The Interview – Billy Laninovich	76
Twelve.	Basketball	86
Thirteen.	Psychologically Speaking	91
Fourteen.	Final Remarks	105

Epilogue   108
Dedication   109
About the Author   111

ACKNOWLEDMENTS

Writing *Youth Sports Are Killing Me Slowly* has been a journey filled with reflection, passion, and purpose. I could not have done it without the unwavering support of my family, friends, and those who have shaped me along the way.

To my wife, Blake—thank you for standing by me through all the crazy ideas I've had over the years. You are my best friend, my partner in crime, and the one who keeps me grounded when life gets chaotic. Your love and support mean everything to me, and I am forever grateful to have you by my side.

To my children, Aislynn and Ezra—you are my greatest inspiration. Without you, I would not be the man I am today. Watching you grow into the incredible young woman and man you are becoming fills me with immeasurable pride. I hope that sports have instilled in you the resilience, discipline, and character needed to succeed in whatever paths you choose in life. No matter where your journeys take you, know that I will always be your biggest fan.

To my parents, Sheri and Warren Seevers—thank you for always believing in me, even when I was a pain in the butt. Your love, guidance, and support have shaped me in ways I can never fully express. I am endlessly grateful for the values you instilled in me and the unwavering encouragement you have given me throughout my life.

To everyone who has supported me along the way—whether through conversations, encouragement, drinking a beer on the beach, or simply believing in this project—thank you. This book is more than just words on a page; it's a reflection of the experiences, challenges, and triumphs that shape all of us in the world of youth sports.

With gratitude,
Cody Seevers

PROLOGUE

This book is not just about my story. It's about the reality of youth sports today, told through the experiences of parents, coaches, and even professional athletes who have lived it. It's about the sacrifices we make, the dreams we chase, and the toll it takes on our families.

I wrote *Youth Sports Are Killing Me Slowly* because I know I'm not alone. If you've ever questioned whether all of this is worth it, if you've ever worried about the pressures on your child, or if you've ever wondered how we got here—this book is for you.

INTRODUCTION

I had just completed what was arguably the most stressful week of my adult life. My 9-year-old son had just had seven tryouts in five days for three different club hockey teams in the southern Boston region. I spent what felt like an exhausting 40 hours on the phone, speaking with the team he's been playing with for the past three seasons, the goalie's dad (a good friend of mine), and countless other parents. We were all trying to figure out the missing pieces in the team's availability to ensure our kids were placed on the best possible team with a coach we could all support. I also called the coaches of the new teams he tried out for.

Three offers came in, and now it was decision-making time. What team do you put your kid on to give them the best chance to succeed?

While my thoughts continued to speed by at a mile a minute, I caught myself. What in the absolute fuck was I doing? The kid is 9 years old, and I am treating these tryouts like he is getting drafted into the NHL. He can't even lace up his own skates!

My name is Cody Seevers, I am 37 years old, and, like my son, I was an athlete throughout childhood and well into adulthood.

I have two kids who are amazing and special in their own ways. My 14-year-old daughter is an outstanding singer and songwriter who loves singing, acting, and playing the guitar. My son loves everything about sports and playing with his friends. I share these incredible kids with the most amazing woman in the world, whom I have been married to for 16 years.

After the stressful week I began discussing this book, I started looking for guidance on how to navigate youth sports. Honestly, I felt like I really struck out with locating the information to keep me grounded and not go over the top, as most parents unintentionally do. So, I told myself that I was going to write the book I was desperately looking for. I knew that if I helped even one parent, I would feel as if I did my part.

So here I am.

My intentions with this book are to showcase the craziness that has surrounded youth sports, from the pressure that we are putting on our kids at such a young age, to the obvious conclusion that we are all living vicariously through our kids while wanting them to avoid some of the failures or mishaps that we may have faced growing up.

Buckle up—youth sports are intense, chaotic, and sometimes downright unbelievable. This is my unfiltered experience as a parent caught in the middle of it all.

CHAPTER ONE

Where It All Started

I grew up in a small town in Southern California called Ramona, which has not changed at all since I relocated almost 17 years ago. It is the kind of town where, on any given day, you may see a horse walking down a dirt road or a dirt bike ripping up the hillside .

This town was very country for being in Southern California.

Football was huge on Friday nights, and just about the whole town shut down business to go to the game and cheer on the home team. "For as big as football was, wrestling was even bigger, with Thursday night dual meets drawing massive crowds. When the lights went out and the music played, the home crowd formed a tunnel for us to run through before our warmups."

Having been part of both of these teams, I know the feeling was exhilarating. If I think long and hard, I can go right back to that moment and hear, smell, and see all of it in slow motion.

I was a kid who was pretty good at almost everything I put my mind to. I played youth football through all the divisions growing up—in my hometown, we called it 'Pop Warner.' I played positions on both sides of the ball, holding the positions of quarterback, running back, and linebacker throughout my time. I can confidently say I was also a coach's dream. I would do anything and everything they asked, and I was never afraid to give or receive a hit.

As I reached my first year in high school, everyone grew except for me. My hopes and dreams of continuing to play quarterback started slipping away, and the spot I thought I earned through my hard work growing up was given to a six-foot-tall kid with a pitching past. Don't get me wrong, the kid could throw a laser and had the height to see over the offensive line. I knew in my heart that it was the best decision for the team, but it didn't make it any easier to accept a new role that I did not want.

I went to my coach and spoke to him about my struggles. For the first time. I was worried about finding a place on this new team, which was a new feeling for me.

My coach was an outstanding man and a great football coach. He was clearly an athlete in his day and worked his ass off to become a successful business owner. He found a way to balance running a successful business by day and coaching football by night. I always thought he could relate to me a bit, because he was not the biggest man on the field, but he had the same burning passion that I did—something you cannot teach. That passion is something you are born with and lives inside you.

We will talk about that more later.

After the discussion, my coach and I decided that I would play cornerback and return punts and kickoffs. I accepted this new role and dove headfirst into it. Although I was unhappy with these new positions as my primary responsibility, I knew that if I did not accept them, there would likely be no starting spot for me on the team.

In my new role. I told myself I wouldn't be happy if I didn't get an interception every single game. As you can imagine, I was often unhappy because my expectations were a bit unreasonable; however, I got several throughout the season and had some very successful kick returns. Looking back on it from an adult's perspective, I wish I hadn't taken the decision so seriously and had just enjoyed playing the game I loved with my friends.

After football season ended, it was right into wrestling season for me. I started wrestling in seventh grade and quickly fell in love with the sport. It was something that I could get instant results from. What kid doesn't like that?

For those of you who have never seen a "Folkstyle" High School wrestling match, there would be a winner or loser within six minutes if you do not go into overtime. Which, compared to most other sports, is an extremely fast turnaround for results. I have always been a very results-driven; when I want something, I want it yesterday.

I began wrestling after my mom introduced the idea to me. At the time, she worked as a security guard for the school, so she had to work sporting events. She went to a Varsity wrestling match and said it had me written all over it.

I had back-to-back winning seasons in my first and second years and was asked by the head coach to attend the varsity wrestling practices over the summers.

During those summers, I surrounded myself with some of the most accomplished wrestlers that Ramona High had ever seen. These individuals always displayed 110% effort from the time practice started until the final whistle blew.

It was during this summer that I got to witness firsthand what a winning mentality looked like physically. I could internalize the effort that they were putting forth, compare it to others who weren't at their level, and make a personal decision about where I would like to be. I have never seen someone push themselves so close to their breaking point repeatedly, so that their bodies get used to operating at this level of fatigue. I knew if I wanted to be as good as them, what I just witnessed in front of me was what I would have to replicate.

After two summers of hard work, the varsity head coach approached me again going into my freshman year. He told me that the effort and determination he saw from me reminded him of a seasoned veteran, and if I kept it up there was going to be a spot open on the varsity team for me.

After hearing this news, I became more focused than I had ever been in my life up to this point. Reaching my goal of earning that spot on the varsity team my freshman year became my everything.

The way it worked was that the team was selected by wrestle-offs, meaning any week, you could challenge or be challenged for your spot on the varsity team. It would consist of a full match which the head coach would referee. The winner would be granted the starting spot on the varsity team.

I prepared and trained all summer long—in addition to playing freshman football—and the day the wrestle-offs came, I didn't care who was on the mat with me. I knew that I would beat them, and I did just that.

I was given the Varsity singlet and warmups that you would wear to school on the day of the dual meet. I will never forget how big I felt walking to class as a freshman in the varsity warmups. In fact, the feeling stayed with me all season. Wearing the warmups symbolized more than just making the team; it was a payoff for all the hard work I had put in. It was the reward at the end of the race. It also served as a reminder for me that this was only the first part. Now, I had to go out there and compete against another team's best.

I don't know what my record was that first year, but I started every single varsity match then and the three years to follow. In my first year, I took third place in the California Interscholastic Federation (CIF) tournament, making it to the Master's tournament but falling short of qualifying for the State Championships by just a few places.

After the wrestling season, the football coach asked me if I was coming back out for the team. At the same time, the wrestling coach was preaching to me about my potential as a wrestler. I ultimately decided to put all other sports on hold to focus on wrestling.

Looking back as an adult, the only reason I can think of for focusing on wrestling was that I was a Varsity Letterman as a freshman, and it was unknown what I would be the following year for other sports.

With wrestling, height and weight did not matter as much; you were always going to face someone who weighed the same as you. This is why they have weight classes in wrestling.

The other thing that went into it was the simple fact that I was really good at it. It came to me fairly easily, and I knew that if I put effort into it, I could be really good—maybe even one of the best.

The other sport that was put on hold during my high school days was racing dirt bikes, which ran through my veins. Looking back on it now, I wish I had played football, wrestled, played golf, and raced motorcross. But I am an obsessive person, and I constantly channel all my energy into one thing at a time, striving to become the best I can be at it.

After making the decision to focus entirely on wrestling, I went and trained with the CAL State Bakersfield team for a week that summer. Qualifying for the State Championship was the ultimate goal, and getting that State patch on your letterman's jacket was the iconic visualization of success.

I won a lot during my junior and senior years, and finally, I qualified for the state championships before graduating. I took second place in all of Southern California and went into the state championship with extreme confidence.

Even though I didn't place at the State Championships, I achieved my high school career goal of making it to Bakersfield and competing in a stadium where you had to purchase tickets on Ticketmaster. It was as incredible as I imagined it would be.

After my season, I was awarded the most varsity-winning record of Ramona Wrestling history, winning well over 100 varsity matches. Looking back at it, I had more in me. I left some on the table, and it will haunt me forever.

In short, there was never an off-season in wrestling, but when we were not competing, our training regimen would change for the worse. We would go to parties and drink, smoke, dip, and do all sorts of "things" that we thought were cool at the time, but they played a massive role in my training. You cannot go out and binge drink, smoke two packs of cigarettes, and dip all night long for months at a time and then expect to get back into shape when competition starts back up. It is just not feasible.

This is one of my regrets in life. I wish I had more oversight and structure during those high school years to keep me more grounded, focusing on my academics and not copying work from my fellow classmates the morning an assignment was due. I wish I had known how important living a healthy lifestyle is, even at a young age, and what the consequences of binge drinking and smoking play on your life and mental health.

I hope that by sharing my experiences, I can help you support your child through the challenges of high school—challenges that can be incredibly difficult to navigate alone.

Last section on me before I move on. I grew up with a family that loved to camp. We had a motorhome for as long as I can remember, spending weekends at Glamis or Gordons Wells (sand dunes in Southern California). Riding quads, dirt bikes, and a dune buggy was a way of life there, and my family loved it. My dad would take my sister, cousins, and me on early-morning "scavenger hunts" to find things the drunk wanderers lost overnight—some of our finds were pretty cool.

I started young, riding a quad at three and getting my first dirt bike at seven. With no way to gauge my skill, my family took me to Barona Oaks (local race track) for my first race.

I won, and from that moment, I was hooked. Racing became my passion; I worked hard to balance it with football and school.

Growing up on five acres, my dad built me a motocross and supercross-style track, so I practiced daily, often until my mom flashed the porch light for dinner.

After high school wrestling ended, I even gave myself a year to see if I could make a career out of racing. I cleaned pools to fund my weekends at the track, entering as many local races as possible, hoping for sponsorships to offset costs.

Despite my dedication, I ultimately fell short of turning motocross into a career.

This was a hard pill to swallow at the time, and I laugh at myself now, thinking that at the age of nineteen, I told myself that I was too old to continue this pipe dream. In reality, I had several more years left to prove I could have made it in the professional ranks.

However, like I said before, I am wired differently. I moved to the next chapter in my life, and if it were not for that decision, I would not have my wife or kids to this day.

Isn't it funny how life unfolds exactly as it's meant to—yet we still cling to the illusion that we're in control?

Where It All Started

10 YOUTH SPORTS ARE KILLING ME SLOWLY...

CHAPTER TWO

The Passion

Since he was about three years old, my son has told me that he wants to become a professional hockey player. I am sure that at some point or another, all of you have heard your son or daughter say something similar. The only problem is that he has a dad like me, who says, "Okay, if this is what you want, then I am going to go all in and help you achieve your goals."

What I don't consider is that the kid is three when he tells me this. So, what do I do?

Probably the same thing that you all did, or you wouldn't be reading this.

You sign them up for 'learn to play hockey' at the closest rink with the soonest availability. Am I right? Maybe you took advantage of the Boston Bruins program and signed up to get all the gear and the four lessons associated with it for a ridiculously low price. I know I did.

The point I am trying to make is that we dive headfirst into a world of youth sports that we don't know.

Maybe you were lucky enough to play the same sports as your child growing up, and you know all the ins and outs. Do you really know the other side of it? The parent side? I think we all end up just diving in.

My son ended up having a blast on the ice, even though he could barely stand up. He thought he was Brad Marchand out there—a very popular NHL star for anyone not familiar. I could care less at the time how he was doing; the kid was happy and loved every second of it.

I understood the emotions that he was feeling because I remember feeling like that when I was a kid, too. You don't know all the politics of the youth sports world and the dysfunction that lies ahead. To kids, this is the first step to the long road of being an athlete, and it very well could be dads like us who ruin that feeling for the rest of their lives.

My son continued to do the learn to play program, which I believe was only a few months, and also completed the Boston Junior Bruins program before moving on to a follow-up session.

Before I knew it, I found myself and my three-year-old at the rink two days every week, learning how to skate from a figure skating coach. She was brilliant and had probably been skating for nearly half a century. Although he enjoyed it mostly, he didn't have his stick in his hand, so that was very short-lived. He was ready to be on a team.

At this point in the story, he was probably approaching the age of four, so we signed him up for the local town's 'mini-might's' team. He got the team jersey, and was able to start practicing with other kids his age, skating around and swarming the puck like bees on honey.

My father-in-law would constantly remind me that these are the years you will never forget because once the kids get older, the game changes, and the innocence goes away. I feel like I tried to take his advice—I really did—but deep down, I knew that I wanted him to be the best kid on the team, score the most goals, and be the fastest skater—all things that were completely irrelevant to the circumstances for development in any sport.

The fact is, passion is what keeps kids motivated, not the parent. It is our job as parents to foster passion and desire in our kids, to keep any sport they are involved in fun, and not put undue stress on them from the age of four. From the conception of him playing hockey, I had to struggle not to ruin him before anything even got started.

He continued with town hockey, and at the end of that year, his team was asked to play in between periods at one of the Providence Bruins games.

Up until this point, this was a once-in-a-lifetime experience for him—to skate in that environment and feel the crowd's presence all around him. The cheering in the stands with the commentator in the distant background is something that will live inside him for his entire existence. I know that to this day, I still remember playing at the halftime show for the San Diego Charges in Pop Warner football. There are so many times I can just feel the sheer emotions that opportunities like this present to young athletes.

After completing his first real hockey season, we looked to figure out what the next year would look like. I had spoken to some different parents to get their opinions and had some family ties to the sport as well—my nephew was playing club hockey with a local organization. After hearing about his experience, we decided to try club hockey the following year. My son has played on a club team ever since.

My son did two years on half-ice and then made his way into playing full-ice with offsides and icing calls. The teams he has been a part of have had some great runs. The first full-ice season, they fell short in the semifinals, ending their season a week earlier than expected.

The funny thing about that was that it later came out that the team we lost to in the semifinals (which we had beaten a few times in the regular season) brought in a few ringers for the playoffs who put on other kids' jerseys so that they wouldn't get noticed.

This was one of my first indicators of how brutal this sport—and all youth sports—can get.

The kids' were crushed at the loss, and there was not much we could do because it was all assumptions with no physical proof. So, we hung that season out in the past and moved on. The following season, they won the overall championship in the Premier Hockey League.

The plot thickens at the start of the first full-ice season. I personally felt that the team dynamic was really strong. We had some great players, and the kids were getting into a groove with their passing skills. However, we had a few players (one in particular) who would never pass the puck.

I will admit it was a bit annoying. Nobody likes a ball-hog. For the most part, we were starting to see these kids work together and get the job done. Heck, we only lost to a good team from Canada in the finals at a tournament by one goal, which was a pretty good outcome given the circumstances.

Undenounced to me, other parents weren't happy as we approached the end of the season. Our coaching staff was going to be split up because the head coach's son was a year behind my son, so he could stay with the younger age group for one more year. That meant a new coach as we headed to the older team.

I have always hesitated with coaches, and, as you will read later, I believe you always follow the coach, not the organization. I ended up emailing the organization once I heard the news to ask what the plan was for coaching the following season. I did not particularly like the answer that I got back. They said something to the effect that they have it under control, and the person they have identified to be taking over is a great coach, and I will be happy. I don't know about you, but I like making my own decisions about whether I will be satisfied.

So, I took my son to tryouts (which fell only around one week after the prior season ended), and there were only nine kids in total there. Out of those nine, only three were returning players. This is when the panic set in.

I am a pretty outgoing person, and when faced with a situation where I can either sit by myself or talk to someone, I typically talk to someone. As you can imagine, over the past several years I have made a few friends at the rink. One of these was the owner of the neighboring club hockey team located on Cape Cod, Massachusetts.

My wife and I decided to make the move to the other club team with that coach, and subsequently, a few others followed us. My son now had a whole new program to learn, new players to connect with, and new coaches to try to impress. All of this comes with a learning curve.

I'm not sure how this is done in other states, but in our area, the kids play in a tournament called Parity before the season starts. This tournament evaluates the team's skill level in order to place them into the correct division for the following season.

Well, what do you know? Our team put on their big boy pants that weekend and showed up to play. They went undefeated and were moved up to the Premier Hockey League.

The Premier Hockey League was loaded with nine other teams from New England, including some of the best teams from Massachusetts, New Hampshire, and Maine.

The definition of 'travel hockey' just got a lot more real to me. On any given weekend, I would now spend six hours in the car for an hour of hockey.

Other parents bat their eyes and talk down on the travel. They say things like, "I can't believe that you spend your whole weekend driving all over New England watching your kids play sports."

"You know all the things you could do with the extra money you would save without all the travel, hotels, and gas?"

Deep down, I love the travel! There is nothing I want more than for my kid to have the opportunity to play the best teams in the region and have that incredible competition. For you to be the best, first you must beat the best.

If only we could do just that—beat some of these teams. That year, our kids got off to a rough start while dealing with some coaching changes.

Personally, I am continuing to learn more about myself as a youth sports dad, and my son as an athlete, than anything else. We have also gotten closer, the more I push away how competitive I naturally am. That year was my first test; I really had to learn how to be a better cheerleader, even with so many losses. These kids are still in the first decade of their lives, and the only way they measure success is through wins and losses. During that season, I wouldn't change a single thing. I would much rather be the last-place team in the best division than the first-place team in the lower division. There is no growth in the comfort zone, and it is not comfortable in the growth zone.

That season, they were in the growth zone. We had the opportunity to challenge these kids mentally and remind them that, yes, they're a good hockey team and they work hard. But even with all that, better teams are still working even harder out there.

As a culture, we have shifted to handing out participation trophies and ensuring everyone feels included. Well, I am here to tell you that when you get into the workforce, they do not hand this crap out, and that if you do not perform well, you can actually lose your job.

So why are we teaching our kids from such a young age that all we have to do is show up and participate?

Again, as much as we all want to win at everything we do, we need to learn how to lose, accept failure, and use it as a building block for future success.

"Right now, we stay humble and grind!" Coach Paul.

CHAPTER THREE

Parents Are Running Youth Sports

How we act and behave as parents directly reflects how our children will turn out.

If you want your daughter to marry a wonderful man, you must first show her what a wonderful man looks like. You have to treat her mom with the respect you hope her future husband will treat her. You have to parent with both the iron fist and a side of compassion and acceptance.

While attending college, I took a class on criminal profiling with an emphasis on eyewitness testimony in the court of law. What I discovered is that no matter who we are as people, when we come across someone for the first time, we immediately compare them to ourselves. That said, when we see our kids out on the ice, we subconsciously do the same. We compare the skill level of all the other kids to our kids because we know our kids almost as well as we know ourselves. "That kid" can stick-handle better than my kid, he can skate backward faster than my kid, or my kid has way better passes than anyone on this team. I am sure that all of you have had this internal conversation at some point and know exactly what I am talking about.

In addition to the toxic comparisons just stated, during a youth hockey game, everyone in the stands finds it acceptable to act like a total asshole. I have heard things screamed at the players (who are kids, let's not forget), referees, and coaches that, if my son or daughter ever said, I would be mortified. The adults seem to lose complete control of the situation and allow themselves to act in a way that would discredit any organization.

And guess what? Our kids see us doing that. The kids feed off the energy in the room over a bad call, and then compile it with a dirty play that further exacerbates the situation, making nothing better.

Parents, here is my advice; keep your mouth shut!

Watch your kid play the game that he or she loves, and cheer on the entire team as you do. You yelling at the referee isn't going to make him or her change their mind. You telling the opponents' fans that they are dirty isn't going to make them play clean all of a sudden.

You do not have to agree with what happens during a game, but you do need to set an example for the kind of person you hope your future son or daughter will become.

* * *

The other day, I went to a party, and it came at the end of a particularly stressful week. My daughter had just been named the lead in the school play, and of course, there was some pretty extreme drama that led up to the final cast list being revealed. My son had just been benched for almost the whole second period of his last hockey game, and work stressors were at a high.

However, it was Halloween, and I needed to pick my ass up and put everything aside to allow my kids to have a memorable Halloween. I even let my son miss practice to go trick-or-treating. What a concept, right? Let a 9-year-old miss practice to go be a kid and have fun.

Every Halloween, my family heads to my buddies' house. They have a great neighborhood tucked back inside the hills on beautiful Cape Cod—perfect for trick-or-treating. They invite several families over, and we all walk around the neighborhood with beverages in hand while the kids do their thing and have fun.

This particular night, I found myself sitting by myself before we headed out on our walk. I cracked open a beer and was just taking it all in. I surveyed the room and observed about four conversations between over a dozen people. I started listening to each one at a time for a few seconds each. What do you think they were all about?

Youth sports, of course!

"Little Tommy pitches so much better when the mound is this far away from home plate."

"Why is there such a controversy about parents who let their kid play tackle football vs flag football?"

"Jessica is not getting as much playing time as other kids on the varsity team because the coach has his favorites."

"Johnny didn't even make the travel basketball team, even though everyone in the room would agree that he was the best player in the seventh grade, because one of the team dads wanted it to be all the kids from his son's school."

Listening to all these over-the-top conversations, I said to myself, "this is fucking crazy." We are grown adults at a social event, yet all we can talk about is our kids' sports. I had to leave the room.

I walked outside to the large group of kids on the front lawn playing three flags up (a football game). Nothing bothered these kids as the day faded into another Cape Cod sunset.

They were living in the moment, and I was extremely jealous. How often have we thought, 'I wish I could bottle up those kids' energy—if I could, I would be a rich man'? Watching them at this moment, I wished I could bottle up their innocence and keep it for a rainy day when I needed it. I continued watching them play for a little bit and focused on my two kids. They waved to me, smiled, and lived their best lives.

CHAPTER FOUR

Heading to the MLB

While researching material for this book, I had the amazing opportunity to sit down with Nick Vincent (a former MLB pitcher) and talk through my thoughts. I found this conversation so insightful, and learning about his journey from Little League to the Major League was humbling. I also found that Nick and I share a lot of the same values: hard work, generosity, manners, and respect for others, to name a few.

Maybe it's because we both grew up in the small town of Ramona and had parents who taught us how to do more right than wrong in this world.

Either way, I hope you all find this interview to be as enlightening as I did.

* * *

Nicholas James Vincent (born July 12, 1986) is an American-born former professional baseball pitcher. He played high school baseball for our common alumni, the Ramona Bulldogs. After that, he tried out at Palomar Junior College and made the team. Nick spent a few years there before moving his talents to Division I and becoming a Long Beach State Dirtbag. After one season with the Dirtbags, he was drafted and began his professional career.

Nick was drafted by the Padres in the 18th round of the 2008 Major League Baseball draft and made his major league debut in 2012. Over his career, he played for the San Diego Padres, Seattle Mariners, San

Francisco Giants, Philadelphia Phillies, Miami Marlins, Texas Rangers, Minnesota Twins, Atlanta Braves, and Detroit Tigers. Nick played in the MLB for 10 years straight (from 2012 to 2021).

* * *

Cody: Who are you beyond baseball? Tell me without mentioning the sport at all.

Nick: I am an easy-going, humble, competitive, and hard-working kind of guy. My parents raised my brother and me very well. Do good things, good things will happen; do bad things, bad things will happen. I was taught to respect everyone, use proper manners such as "please" and "thank you," and treat people the way you would want to be treated.

I think of myself as a simple man.

Cody: Do you feel that professional athletes are born with God-given talent, or is it something that hard work and determination can overcome?

Nick: I don't think it is God-given talent. Don't get me wrong, there are a lot of professional athletes that are blessed with God-given talent, or maybe they have the genetics that make them stand out as the cream of the crop athletes, all of which puts them ahead of the curve in sports.

When I graduated from high school, I weighed 135 pounds. I was always the smallest kid on my Little League teams. I didn't throw very hard, but I threw strikes with all my pitches. I didn't have above-average pitches to get drafted out of high school, so I took my talents to Palomar Junior College tryouts.

I had to work extremely hard to get my chance to pitch at a Junior College! At every single level, I had to constantly grind my way to the next level. There are sacrifices that you will have to make as a young athlete to make yourself the best player you can. It's a balance—having fun with friends and family and getting your work in to perfect your talents.

Those blessed with the God-given talent don't have to work as hard to be on top initially, but can struggle to stay on top once they are there. Then, you have your superstars who are the ones that are blessed with God-given talent and work extremely hard because they want to be the best of the best.

For example, after high school was over, I didn't know what I was going to do. My father owned his own firewood, tree service, and construction company. So, it was either go do construction with my dad, or try out for baseball. I had a friend who asked if I wanted to join him for a try out at Palomar Junior College. We tried out together, and I wound up making the team.

This is the point in time when I realized that maybe I have what it takes to be competitive. My work ethic and determination from all my years in youth sports, through high school, coupled with the values that my parents instilled into me, were what it took for me. It was not God-given talent.

I took full advantage of any opportunity to showcase what I could offer; I took full advantage of it and gave it my all. In my years coming up through various sports teams, I have found that you only need to impress one or two people. How you conduct yourself, your ability to be coachable, and your demeanor on and off the field go so much further than you realize.

Cody: Did you ever have any coaches who were detrimental to your progression? This could mean sending you backward rather than helping you grow as an athlete.

Nick: You are always going to have both good and bad coaches. Some know how to coach, and some do not.

Sometimes, you get lucky with coaches who do it for the right reasons, such as their love of the game, their desire to see others succeed, or their desire to help the kids be better people going forward. The best coaches are the ones who can do all that and engrave core values along the way. Other times you see people fill that coaching role because they want their kid to be the superstar on the team.

As a young athlete, I never considered good or bad coaches. I thought of it as—I like this coach more than some other coaches I have had. I just played whatever sport I was playing, and tried to be a good teammate, be coachable, and be respectful. If and when you have a bad coach, and your parents start blaming the coach early on, you, as the kid, are almost always going to blame the coach, too.

We as parents need to make sure we do not talk bad about any of our kids' coaches in front of them. It only makes the situation worse. It only fuels our children's fire, which leads to a lack of effort and then a lack of performance.

Instead, treat this as an opportunity to speak to your kids, saying that you will not like everyone in this world. However, in the real world, whether you like someone or not does not change the fact that you are going to have to work with them.

Kids soak up everything you do and will repeat that attitude. A toxic attitude is a terrible attribute to have as a parent. You have to withhold your strong opinions in these situations.

Of course, I would sometimes question a certain coach on things growing up, but in a respectful way. I always had more respect for older coaches with their years of experience and wisdom that they brought to the game. Those old timers were always a blast to play for.

Towards my later years in baseball, I started having coaches who were younger than I was. I always told myself that I would at least try to do what they were asking of me, but if I gave it my best effort and I did not like it or feel comfortable with it, I would go back to the way that felt natural to me because it has gotten me to where I am today. I learned a lot about which coaches will help me the way that I learn best, and which will not.

Whether the parent is dealing with a good or bad coach, it is imperative to remember to be the adult and talk through the situation. Make sure you are in a supporting role in a situation like this because, often, in these instances, your kid isn't pleased with how the season is going.

For example, if you are the parent who critiques your child's performance after every game, the child will most likely lose love for the game. We got a saying in baseball: "We'll get them tomorrow." Sometimes, less is more as a parent. I heard on a podcast one time, "Let the coach's coach. You be the parent."

Don't get me wrong—there are times you could be hard on your child—it builds character. But not every time, especially after they already know they didn't play well.

As a parent, you have to learn to let go of the uncontrollable and teach your child to do the same. No matter the coach, as a young athlete, I would always hustle on and off the field. That way, they see you hustle, and your effort can never be in question, even if you do not see eye to eye on certain things. Every player and parent can only control the controllable. You have to let go of everything else.

Cody: Did you ever have any amazing coaches who you are still thankful for today?

Nick: I have had many great coaches for whom I am fortunate enough to have played. My number one coaches, though, were always my parents. They were there from day one, putting in practice and travel hours after long work days. Engraving a work ethic that I will never lose.

When it comes to traditional coaches, I think of Chris Bertolero as one of my most memorable great coaches. In my freshman year of high school, I didn't make the Freshman team. But Coach Bertolero had seen me playing baseball growing up and knew I was a good player. He knew I had just not had a good tryout.

So, he took me on his JV team as a freshman. I started most games at shortstop and then pitched when our starter wasn't, and he would swap out with me at shortstop. Without Coach Bertolero taking that chance on me, I don't know what would have happened; I might have given up playing baseball.

Another coach who left a lasting mark on me was Bob Vetter (head coach for Palomar Junior College) who was instrumental in the "Baseball theory" part of my game. I was also very fortunate to have Coach Vetter because he brought 30-40 years of baseball and life experience to the table. I appreciated him so much.

I have had so many coaches over the years, and have learned that they all have information that will add value to you and your game. You have to listen to all of it and take the pieces out that you feel will work for you.

"Why did God give you two ears and one mouth? So that you will listen twice as much as you should speak."—Nick Saban.

At the end of the day, there is a good list of coaches I would like to thank for their contributions to my success. Just remember, parents, let your kids have fun!

Cody: When was the point in your amateur career that you first knew that you could make a career out of playing baseball?

Nick: I would say during my first year at Palomar Junior College. I learned a slider towards the end of the year in high school. I was seeing instant success with that pitch. So, I brought that pitch with me to Palomar.

At this point, I wanted to continue to get better and better. I saw what I had accomplished through hard work and trusting the process, and I saw that I could get the ball to move both directions in the strike zone and feel confident in doing so. While at Palomar, the slider reassured me that I could possibly play Division I baseball. Back then, I was confident enough to think I could pitch in the big leagues. Confidence goes a long way in sports and in life.

I took this confidence in pitching to college. Until now, I had not had a structured workout or training program. That changed in college, and proper training became a part of my everyday life.

I became the third starter in the rotation and, just like that, a lightbulb switched. I started the season off way better than I would have ever expected. I was 5-0, with a 1.30 ERA, striking out between seven and ten batters every game. I was even in awe of my success at this point. Unfortunately, I got hurt early on in the season with an elbow injury and took the rest of that season off.

I was so hungry to get back the next year that I worked harder and harder. I came back the following season better and stronger than I had been the previous year. My second season, I went 9-2, and had a 1.51 ERA. I knew if I kept this level of progression, I could go play ball at the Division I level.

I transferred to Long Beach State University at the end of my third season—the Dirtbags! I was even more confident after my time at Long Beach State, where my control continued to develop, and I learned the mental side of baseball.

Cody: How do you define success as an amateur athlete?

Nick: Success comes with hard work, dedication, and finding a way to deal with adversity. Seeing results after all the hard work and hours you put in throughout the year. Early morning workouts, school during the day, practice all afternoon, and conditioning all evening. You have to trust the process and believe in yourself. This does not just happen overnight.

You start throwing harder, running faster, hitting the ball better, and acknowledging that all your work is paying off. It's just like how the Egyptians built the pyramids. They built a solid foundation and continued building and building until they reached the top. All the while, each individual person has a different route to getting to the top.

That's the beauty of sports. Hearing each guy or girl's journey to success. Not everyone has the same growth points while coming up. You have to trust in yourself and trust in the process. The bottom line is that you must work to get where you want to be.

None of us were taught to take our time and trust the process. When you are a professional, you are going to have bad days. Contrary to popular belief, nothing is easier when you reach this level. Some days, you are throwing the ball all over the place. But, you still want to be the best you can be every time you are on the mound.

When you are having these bad days, you need to leverage the healthy experiences you have built in your foundation. You have to believe in yourself and re-engage with the confidence to go out there and do your job.

One of the most important things a parent can do is instill good values and build confidence along the way because these will last a lifetime, whether it is on a sports team or whatever you wind up doing for a living.

Cody: What is the hardest step in going from the amateur to the professional ranks?

Nick: Long Beach State did a fantastic job preparing me for pro ball. Besides my education and playing career, the only gear we received as players was a new glove, a pair of cleats, a reversible jersey, shorts, and a hat. I thought I would be getting some stuff playing for the Dirtbags, but that was not the case. They had a way of teaching their guys grit and how to play hard-nosed baseball.

It ended up being great that they did because I saw the same treatment once I went pro. You might think that when you get drafted, you suddenly get all this free gear, but that is not the case. In fact, I didn't get anything for free until I made the 40-man roster for the San Diego Padres. If you are a first-round draft pick and on the fast track, things might be a little bit different, but for me, I was paying for all of my things. I remember when I was on my first professional contract, I asked a coach if I should get an agent. He snickered a little bit and said that it would be wise to just continue to buy my own stuff and that I should wait a little longer.

The other thing that was hard for me to adjust to was the unknown of how professional baseball will be until you get there. I don't think this is something that really anyone could prepare for.

You have worked your whole life for this, and now that you made it, you have no clue what to expect.

In my first year playing for the Padres Minor League team, they had a team rule that you had to live in the team hotel for the first year and share a room with another player. With all the differences, if I had gone straight from high school to the Minor Leagues, I don't know if I would have made it.

Thankfully, college set me up for success, and I learned the things needed to live with others besides my parents and brother.

You also learn through college how to mature and start becoming an adult, which greatly helped me transition into the minors. So regardless of where you were or where you came from the first year playing professional baseball your living conditions were a big adjustment. Hotel rooms and suitcases, to baseball fields and gear bags, back to hotel rooms and suitcases. Making $400 every two weeks. It was a whirlwind.

During my earlier years, I also learned to be accountable for my time to operate on a schedule. Overall, I went through a lot of growing up, which should be instilled in you by your parents.

You can get fined for showing up late in the big leagues. You could get released if it happens often. If you got released from a team because of something like this, you can pretty much kiss your chances of continuing in the league goodbye. The message you're sending to the organization is that you don't care to be there if you're always late.

Thankfully, my dad always said, "Time is money." That was engraved in my DNA as I spent many years working in construction with him, and it stuck with me into pro ball. We were always to the job early and had everything prepared to start the workday. That's how I wanted my baseball career to be as well.

Cody: Do you believe parents can ruin a career before it even starts?

Nick: Yeah, of course. There are a lot of parents who push their kids way too hard early on. They are trying to do the best for their kids, but they actually do the opposite. There's this thing called FOMO (Fear of Missing Out). A lot of parents are going through this more now than ever before. There are too many options and opinions on what your kid does at an early age, and most parents feel the pressure of not giving their kid every opportunity.

They can also be too hard on their kids at times, which builds up in a child until they eventually lose it. Let them have fun with what they are doing. Let them be kids.

Overbearing parenting in sports will ruin a kid's love for that sport faster than their failure at it would. Don't have them out there for three hours before practice, getting extra training in. Instead, let them ride their bike around the block for some extra activity. Let them experience the things that kids should be doing—combining their daily physical activity with fun and friends.

My Daughter dances four days a week, and she loves it. I won't make her practice more; four days a week is plenty of time. The rest of her time should be spent being a kid and having fun, building healthy memories that will last a lifetime.

As her parent, I also want to have a special relationship with her. I compare raising children at all different ages to raising them as babies. When kids wake up in the morning, they are so happy and will joyfully hang out for a few hours, play, and have fun. Then, they eat some lunch and go down for a nap. Then the evening arrives, which can be a slippery slope.

This applies to all youth, in my opinion. Maybe they have been at school all day, and maybe it wasn't a great day for them. Then, young athletes go straight from school to practice and are there for a couple of hours. Maybe because they had a bad day at school, their head is not fully in the practice and they have a bad time. At the end of this long day, the last thing they want to hear is how you think they weren't trying their hardest and could have done better.

You have to know your child, and then see what kind of coaching they need from you that day.

Cody: How hard did your parents push you?

Nick: Looking back, I don't think they pushed me too hard, but then again, I was a child. I didn't know any different. I actually got pushed harder working for my dad than in sports. My dad would practice with my brother and I after work, but it was required for me to work from a really young age. I have been splitting firewood and doing construction from as far back as I can remember. Playing baseball after all of this was fun to me. My post-work treat and my light at the end of the tunnel on some long days. My dad definitely gave me the work ethic that molded me into being successful at whatever task was in front of me.

I do remember one time during little league, my dad was shouting at me from the bleachers, telling me how to pitch. I don't know where it came from, but I was giving it my all and I barked back from the mound telling him to leave me alone. He backed off and let me pitch.

I think that was when he decided to let me start doing stuff myself. I feel like in that situation, it was a mutual exchange of respect that was agreed upon. He knew I was a competitor, and I would always compete my tail off on the baseball field.

Cody: You are married and a parent now. What is your and your wife's parenting approach to sports with your kids?

Nick: Truthfully, we haven't gotten too deep into that conversation. We live in Austin, Texas, now, where sports are massive. That said, even without the discussion, I know I will not be a crazy sports Dad.

I want my kids to play at whatever skill level they will get the most playing time and have the most fun. We will explore that path if they are good enough to play on a traveling team. But if they are not, they will play at whatever level it is so that they get to experience all the joys of sports.

Part of the growth that sports can give you is actually related to building confidence. If you are playing in a division that is further along than you are, you will not build confidence as an athlete. In fact, you will probably go the other way—creating doubt and fear.

If you are always sitting on the bench on a travel team, you shouldn't be there. Have your child play at a level where they can play every game and get the reps they need to get better each time. This should also help them grow as a person at each level.

Cody: Do you believe that club/travel teams have changed the DNA in youth sports?

Nick: Yes, and it is sad to see in today's day. The world of youth sports has truly become a business.

People can make a lot of money coaching a club team. When I was growing up, there were only a handful of club teams, and I never played on any of them because I worked during the summer with my dad. That was never a priority for my family. All I ever knew was to play recreational baseball (little league), making all-star teams, and then playing high school baseball. Looking back now, it sounds much simpler when I was coming up.

Cody: What do you think about parents having their younger children (pre-teens) attend private lessons or spend multiple days a week at the practice facility?

Nick: I think it is good and bad, but you can't and shouldn't rely on it as the sole focal point of their progression. If you are going to do private lessons, you have to be there as a parent listening to what the coach is saying so that when you go home, you can emphasize what the coach was teaching.

From time to time, I will do private pitching lessons in my community, and I will get parents who drop their kids off and say, "Okay, I'll be back in an hour." Parents should be there; you need to listen and help go over it at home. In my opinion, the parent has to spend time with their kid to help them get better. You are part of your child's journey, so you might as well make it impactful.

Cody: What did you prioritize in your amateur career, and what were your goals as you climbed the sports ladder?

Nick: My dad said it very early on, and it stuck with me for my entire career; "Just throw strikes." So that was my goal growing up, and he was right. I saw success when I threw strikes and failure when I did not.

Goals change the farther along you get in your playing career. Achieve one goal and then set new goals. I knew that if I was able to play Division I baseball at a high level, I would have a chance to get drafted and live out every boy's dream.

Cody: What were some of your bad habits or what would you change looking back?

Nick: I didn't have too many bad habits as a young athlete, but a few come to mind. Sometimes, I would stay up too late, not giving my body enough time to recover. This is something that is important at any age as an athlete, younger or older. In college, I learned more about recovery than ever before, which helped a lot with knowing what to prioritize in my training.

Also, it would be hard to shake things off early in my career after a bad game. This one took time for me, and it does for most athletes. However, finding ways to deal with adversity is imperative in the world of athletics.

Cody: Any words of wisdom you would like to share with any coach, parent, or young person reading this book?

Nick: Oh wow, where do I start?

Raise your kids to be good human beings, and teach them to be coachable. Ensure they listen to others (especially adults) and appreciate what they tell them. Encourage them to say please and thank you, sir, and ma'am.

Having respect is so important.

Coaches will be more willing to teach your child if these things are instilled early on in their lives. If your child has a bad attitude and is not willing to listen, most coaches will not even waste their time with them. It's sad to say, but it's true, and I just want to make sure all parents know of the importance of instilling respect in our young athletes.

Finally, don't try to be a coach from the stands when you are at your child's games. Let the coaches coach. Just stand back and watch the game. Things will end up being mentally easier for your child and yourself once you get comfortable with this.

*　*　*

After hearing his full story—from early influences to life in professional baseball—I was left reflecting on the depth of experience, humility, and insight he carries with him—insight that offers valuable perspective for any adult involved in the world of youth sports.

I find it fascinating that Nick was instilled with a hard work ethic from a young age that ended up being carried over into his sports as he was progressing through the various different levels in baseball.

Teaching our children how to be hard workers could very well be the key to long-term success.

Also, this interview made it clear that Nick's Father displayed the type of leadership that was 'leading by example.' He taught Nick to be the first to the job site, and to be prepared for a long, hard day's work. He taught Nick that he could go play baseball only when all of his chores and responsibilities were done.

This leadership is long lost in the current era of parenting. Parents nowadays (myself included from time to time) tend to do more of the chores around the house to allow our kids to focus more on school and sports. Whereas, when Nick was growing up, there was no expectation that sports would come before school and chores.

There is a large correlation between teaching children how to be hard workers and do well in school, and their performance as young athletes and their eventual growth into functioning adults.

During his interview, I also noted that Nick never played on a club sports team. Instead, he played on the town and school teams. This, in my opinion, led to Nick's community-first approach and building long-lasting friendships that would last from an early age all the way through senior year in high school.

Building these relationships on and off the field not only supports a child's overall development but also significantly improves their ability to work together as a team during games. If you know a lot about your team, then you really know how to motivate and be a good teammate when things are not going your way.

Another section that stuck out to me was when Nick shared a story about a time when his dad was trying to tell him how to pitch a certain way, and Nick spoke up for himself during the game. I think his actions in this scene are such a valuable take away from this interview because every kid is going to come to a certain age when they know what needs to get done, and they know how to do it.

If you teach your children how to be confident and trust in themselves, then, just like in Nick's story, where he tells his dad he has it under control, there will come a moment when they show you they're ready. At which, as parents, we need to take this as a gift and realize that our child is advocating for themselves and has the confidence to do so. They know what they need to do to complete whatever task. We parents might just see this situation as a single event where our children turn from young boys and girls to young men and women.

The last thing I will reflect on is that being coachable and likeable goes much further than we realize. For example, Nick talks about giving 100% effort during practice, even when he did not get along with a certain coach that well, because he knew that effort is something that only he is responsible for.

At several points in this interview, you could tell Nick was one of the players who was liked in the bullpen. He was respected by his coaches. If push comes to shove, and a coach has to decide whether you stay or leave, being likeable and coachable over someone who is a "know it all" could very well be the reason you stay somewhere or have to move on down the road.

I also believe that this is one of the greatest life skills anyone can acquire. Being a good friend, putting family and friendships ahead of the things that do not matter in a year or ten years. These are the things that we need to be teaching our kids. Being a good person is much more advantageous in the "game of life" than just defying yourself as a good athlete.

CHAPTER FIVE

Coaches Are Not Perfect

'A person who teaches and trains the members of a sports team and makes decisions about how the team plays during games'—that is the dictionary definition of a coach. Please take note that it states the word "person." Coaches are not robots, perfect people, or unicorns from the stars. They are everyday people, just like you and me.

With coaches, parents tend to be very quick to judge when they do something they disagree with. One of a coach's biggest hurdles is YOU, us, parents. We play a substantial role in the stress we put on our coach—and it's up to us whether we help ease it or make it worse.

The stress that parents put on coaches is not the only factor in this equation. Coaches are often also parents, spouses, employees, and human beings. Like the rest of us, they juggle personal and professional responsibilities while trying to lead, teach, and inspire our children. It's easy to forget that behind the whistle is someone managing their own life, with their own pressures and challenges.

Also, like all people, coaches are not perfect and will make mistakes. What most parents want to see out of a coach is their shoulder your child can cry on and their boot up your ass when needed. You need a well-balanced mix of stern but fair. Coaches must be able to inspire their athletes, and hold them accountable, all of which is an extremely difficult task when you put into perspective all of the other influences that they have in their personal lives.

Another key difference with coaches to remember is when your son or daughter plays town sports versus club sports. Little Jonny's dad or mom may be the coach when you play town sports. Most likely, they have little to no prior coaching experience. But they are there on time and ready to do the best job with the skills they have. They get paid nothing, and they volunteer too many hours answering questions late at night, setting the schedule up, giving rides to practice and games, etc. Honestly, the list goes on and on.

Having said that, your expectations of a town sports coach must be far less than those of a club sports coach. Town sports do not turn kids away from participating; they will always find a spot on the team.

When you sign up for a club team, your expectations of the coach should also rise. If you are paying several thousand dollars a year, you expect your coach to have a serious sports background in the field your child is playing in. For example, the coach has a method to their practice schedule and shows up with a plan each day. The expectation is that they played extremely competitive sports at a pretty high level, and they exemplify composure while displaying the characteristics of a professional.

As parents (and coaches), it is important to remember that we are trying to raise good humans, not only be the best youth sports team. My son has been coached by a few former NHL players, but he has also been coached by a regular dad.

I can't put a finger on who was better.

They both brought valuable skills to the table that were essential in my sons' development. The most important quality to look for in a coach is that they are a good person—someone who will instill strong values in your child and push them to become the best version of themselves.

* * *

Some kids have a tough time fitting in. Everyone has a different upbringing, which means cultural differences and knowledge-based examples that set them apart. There are never going to be the same two kids on any one team. The ability to work cohesively is what makes a team successful and what makes a coach capable of achieving success.

A team's (and a coach's) success also depends on the athlete's attitudes. It only takes one sour apple to make a whole team suffer. One kid in the locker room acting out and not paying attention can have a serious ripple effect on the organizational structure.

Often, we hear young athletes say, "Coach doesn't like me." I do not believe that a coach just has it out for a kid. What I do believe is the following:

Coaches don't like:

1. A lack of effort
2. Showing up late for practice
3. Talking when they're talking
4. Being ineligible to play due to poor academic performance.
5. Not following instructions
6. Asking to be put in the game
7. Poor sportsmanship
8. Lack of skill development
9. Talking back
10. Talking trash about teammates

If you're doing any of those, it's your behavior they don't like, not you as a person.

Parents need to take more responsibility for this. If you expect your child to be one of the starters, knowing that they are good players and deserve the role, but they are no longer playing the amount of time you feel they should, have a conversation with your child before asking the coach why your son or daughter is not playing as much as the others.

Ask your child about their behavior. Ask them if they are behaving and listening in the locker room. Watch them during practice, and make sure that when it was their turn at the front of the line, they didn't look like they didn't know what to do because they were not paying attention to the direction given.

Tell your child that every practice should be treated like a try-out, and that if they want to be in the starting line-up, they need to identify themselves as the one the coaches can count on and be the team leader. There is no age too young to teach your child how to be a leader; remember that the best way to lead is by example.

Any coach would choose a kid who is coachable and willing to put in the work over a player with a ton of skill who is lazy and does not pay attention. The player who works hard and is ready to perform can easily develop the skill over time and will, in return, be a much better player overall.

As a parent, having a relationship with your child's coach is extremely valuable, even if you do not agree with everything. The ability to have an open conversation with your child's coach is a really important thing. You do not have to be best friends with the coach, but there needs to be effort put towards this relationship.

Have you ever experienced a back-to-school night where you talked to your child's teacher and heard they are having a hard time or are being disruptive to the class? The teacher and the parent then devise a plan to enforce rules at school, with the plan to implement those same rules at home. The theory here is that the child is learning that the expected behavior is not only something that has to take place at school but also in the home. This is a two-tier approach where the teacher and the parent work together to reinforce the learning objective to achieve a better overall outcome for the child's success.

Why should this be any different in sports?

For example, suppose your child's coach and you do not agree on playing style, and you have been telling our child that they should be doing it one way while the coach is telling them to do it another way. In that case, it becomes extremely confusing for the child to know what they should be doing at any given point. They want to listen to you because you are their parents, and they want to listen to their coach because they are the coach. This is a recipe for a disaster.

In this situation, the parent should recognize that the coach is the coach for a reason, and your child should be doing it the way the coach wants it to be done.

You, as parents, may ask the coach, "What strategies should I be reinforcing at home so that we are reading off of the same sheet of music?" By doing so, you are not only forming a trusting relationship with the coach, but also teaching your child how to build a healthy relationship. You are leading by example by collaborating with the coach and coming up with a strategy for progression.

The coach sees you putting in the work outside of standard practice with your child and knows that their values are being acknowledged. This helps build trust in your child as a player when it comes down to making a game-time decision. Now, your child might very well find themselves as the one that the coach puts in the game.

CHAPTER SIX

Referees Don't Get Paid Enough

I recently read an article about how hard it is to find referees nationwide and across all sports. The article proposed some solutions, including some ideas about implementing different-colored zebra strips for those under the age of 18.

The reason behind this was that they feel that if a 15-year-old was out refereeing and they had a different-colored uniform on, the parents in the stands would be able to identify their young age, feel sympathetic, and therefore not yell at them as much as usual. I personally think it is a brilliant idea and would stand behind this until the end.

Regardless if you think this is a good idea or not, how shitty is it that we have to have this conversation in the first place? As a parent at some of my son's games, I've witnessed grown men shouting at the top of their lungs at a referee, who is out there alone, likely earning no more than $50, and may only be 16 years old.

They accuse the referee of being "blind" and missing numerous calls. I know I would lose it if I ever heard a grown man talk like that to my kids at that age.

Then what, us parents turn a blind eye because we are so uber competitive that we think our shouting is worth it? It's really disappointing when parents exhibit poor behavior in youth sports. If you're one of those people, you must check your ego and rethink your actions. It doesn't reflect well and only makes you seem like someone struggling with personal issues. Let's all focus on supporting the kids and fostering a positive environment.

Again, our conduct is a direct reflection of how we should expect our children to behave.

This also applies to the coaches. Parents should always position their child in a way that follows the coach, not the players, or even the organization. If you (as parents) see your coach yelling at any referee at a young age in competitive sports, you need to consider what that message is telling your young athlete.

When I was wrestling, my father always told me that there were three components in the match: me, my opponent, and the referee. He said, "Don't ever put yourself in a situation for the referee to have to make a call that you are not okay with." What he meant was, "Just go out there and do your job, and then it won't matter what referee is out there."

*　*　*

If I were to guess why people in the stands treat referees so poorly, I'd say it's because they're often caught up in their own frustrations. Maybe they have a long commute, dislike their boss, or feel like they're being controlled at home. Whatever the reason, they unload all their pent-up frustration on that poor referee when a bad call is made.

I would also bet my next paycheck that these same people are the worst drivers the roads have ever seen. Negativity is the same as quicksand; if you surround yourself with others who are also negative, you will slowly start to sink into it, and it will begin to consume your life. You will turn into a person who looks at the glass as half-empty, instead of half-full.

You'll be the one who can't enjoy watching your child play a game, simply because they love it, even if they're not the best at it, but they're having fun. You will begin to put blinders up from reality, and have such tunnel vision with your foresight on yourself (not your child), that you will ultimately ruin your child's passion and motivation for sports in general.

CHAPTER SEVEN

Managing the Stress as a Parent

In today's day and age, things are different. 180-degrees different from when I was playing sports, and another 180-degrees different from when my parents were involved in sports. But that doesn't mean we are right back to where we were half a century ago. Instead, it means we are in uncharted waters, which is all new.

The stress and anxiety that I have developed as a parent of a young athlete are not okay. I have put myself into a situation where the conventional thought process is not what I am doing. I have found myself trying to 'keep up with the Joneses,' for lack of better words.

If one parent is going to send their kid to this summer hockey camp, I have to send my kid, or he will be at a competitive disadvantage. I am willing to go into work early, not take a lunch, and work straight through my day so that I can get off at a reasonable time to pick my son up and bring him to a hockey camp in the middle of July and August. My wife thinks I'm nuts half the time, and always has a private conversation with our son to make sure that he really wants to do it before she signs off on it.

Is all this travel, clinics, and club sports the right thing I should do?

Well, I approach it a bit differently. I do ask my son if this is what he wants to do. Again, my son loves the sport and has turned out to be quite the competitor—he has become a dual threat, with coaches knowing they can play him on offense or defense because he is smart and knows the game well. He is also mature and not the crazy kid in the locker room—we all know that kid—every team has one.

However, some of my actions may show the stress that I feel regarding giving him every opportunity to get on the ice. The craziest part? In the world of youth sports we are in, I am not even the worst offender of this. I heard dads talking about getting their kids up at the crack of dawn for a morning skate before school on Fridays. Mind you, we are still talking about 9-year-olds! As crazy as I can get sometimes, even at my worst, I am still way less crazy than others.

All of this is said because youth sports are killing me slowly.

I used to be an extremely fit guy who ran marathons and competed at a high level. I have slowly allowed myself to go—total dad bod here. I drink a considerable amount of alcohol, use nicotine pouches, and am on the cusp of having high cholesterol, sleep apnea, and have even started taking an anxiety pill a few years back for managing my day-to-day life.

With all of this being said, a significant lesson I have learned is that my attitude and my short temper from time to time are a direct reflection of how I am teaching my kids to behave. After multiple cases of me losing my shit, my wife was ready to kick my ass to the curb if I wasn't willing to go get help. So, help is what I went and got because there is nothing in this world I wouldn't do for my wife and kids. I had to self-reflect on the man I was being and the man I wanted my kids to remember me by. My actions were not from someone I would look up to, and, therefore, changes needed to be made.

Stress is a part of everyone's life. My stress is no more important than your stress, and vice versa. We each deal with stress differently, and a lot of that has to do with our personality type. I am a hard "D" (DISC assessment) on the personality scale. If you have never taken one of these assessments, it is actually a really good thing to do. It is even better to have you and your spouse do it so that you can identify things that work or do not work well with one another. I've challenged myself and educated myself to understand what it takes to push through barriers that, in the past, I wouldn't have been able to overcome.

All the topics we have discussed can come full circle to why our kids play youth sports, which really is the "million-dollar question."

We have our kids participate in sports to learn life lessons. To learn to problem solve with teammates and to work as a team to achieve a common goal. Your child learns that when they are exhausted, they pick themselves up and get it done because someone is counting on them.

I love the acronym T.E.A.M—Together, Everyone, Achieves, More. All of this is applicable in the workforce. The likelihood of becoming a professional hockey player is approximately 0.1%, and, therefore, the reality is that my son will most likely work for the rest of his life. If we do not teach our kids how to contribute to society, then we are nothing more than failures.

One of the big takeaways with youth sports is that if we cannot figure out how to manage our own stress, how can we expect our kids to not have stress in their lives?

In this case, we have basically put it in place for them! As previously mentioned, kids live in the moment and do not see the world in the evil manner that we sometimes do. They likely wouldn't be aware of issues like politics, shootings, or financial struggles if we didn't introduce our own biases and perspectives to them.

I was raised to believe that the President of the United States was the President of the United States, and no matter what you think of him, you will respect him because he is the leader of the free world. Now, we have full-fledged kids in the trenches of the President Trump and Biden debate. We have kids getting into fights about who they think is better. Are any of their arguments information that they took the time to look up, or is it information we have filled their brains with, causing them to get upset if someone disagrees with them, because that would show that Mom and Dad are not right? Basically, it is most likely their little internal mechanism wanting to protect Mom and Dad at all costs.

From birth to sixteen, it is really not okay. My parents never even talked to me about politics—they just lived their lives, voted for whoever they voted for, and moved on. Now, as an adult, I understand their political spectrum, but growing up, I knew no difference. That is the part of innocence we need to protect in our children.

My wife and I try our hardest to only teach the facts about what is going on in the world, with no bias. Instead, our focus is to teach them how to be good and respectful kids, to do more right than wrong in this world, to lend a hand when others need it, and to work their ass off and expect nothing for free as an adult.

* * *

I feel that my kids may have a competitive advantage over most others because of a family decision that my wife and I made a few years back. We were so sick and tired of not being a part of the solution to the problems surrounding us, and so in our own way, we became the solution.

My wife has wanted to be a foster mother since she was a little girl. I remember her talking about it early on in our relationship. I fell in love with her so much because of her genuine and kind nature (it also helps that she is a "10").

We decided that we would do it after we started our own family and had our finances in order with a big enough house to support a foster child. When our kids were six and nine, we felt we were in that place.

We visited the Department of Child and Family Services website and signed up for the lengthy course. This course met once a week on a virtual Zoom call—a result of COVID. We logged on every week for those hours and learned about how to become a foster parent.

This class was the most beneficial class I have ever taken. I honestly think any new parent should take this class because it taught me so many new things. I wish I had some of these new skills while in the trenches with my kids.

That being said, I learned that parenting is much more psychological than we realize. Learning simple skills, like bringing yourself down to the child's level and speaking to them in a really soft voice, is ten times more effective than raising your voice and yelling at them. The moment you have to tell your kid, "Because I'm the boss," you are no longer the boss, just an FYI.

Fathers, especially, can feel that they have to lead with an iron fist. We are the bad cop, and Mom is the good cop. We will be the force of rath, and Mom will be the voice of reasoning.

I've come to realize just how wrong that really is.

Our kids need to know that we as fathers have coping skills, we can listen and not blow up, even though you just told me you shot a puck through my front windshield.

We need to say things like, "Buddy, that must have been hard for you to tell me, but I really appreciate you being honest with me. Do you think that was the best place to play hockey? No, okay, well maybe next time you ask me to move my truck, and I will gladly do so."

How we talk to our children has more impact than you care to believe. Responding to your kids question with things like, "hey you know what, I don't have the answer to your question right now, but I will look into it and get back to you," or, " you have a very creative mind and I would like to think about my response before I give it to you," are incredibly impactful. These are all things that my wife was aware of and knew as a mom, but as a dad, it had not really set in as much as it did when we took that foster class.

Since we took that class, we have probably had over 20 kids come through our home. Some for a whole year, and others for just as little as one night. Every one of these kids has had something in their life that has happened, and they are looking for help. My kids have the biggest hearts and enjoy being a positive role model in these kids' lives. I believe it has taught my kids not to judge a book by its cover and that you never know what someone is going through without asking and truly caring to hear the answer. I believe my wife and I's decision to do foster care will undoubtedly change my kids' lives forever by impacting the woman and man they will become.

* * *

To most people, one of the biggest stressors in life is money. It seems that I am making the same amount of money, yet everything is getting more expensive.

I realize that at this point, I haven't even told you what I do for a living, and that was by design. I wanted to set a good foundation of just me and my thoughts on youth sports (or in my case, youth hockey).

I chose a career path that would allow me to be around many like-minded people who work as a team and are a part of a unit supporting a common goal. A lot of athletes growing up struggle to find their place in life after sports, and I was one of them. So, I did what I thought was the next best thing and joined the Military.

I chose to enlist in the Coast Guard because I really like the mission that the organization supports. At my core, I enjoy lending a hand when someone needs help. And I know I have several shipmates who would help me if I reached out. So, I joined the Coast Guard and worked my ass off for the first decade, gaining as much experience as I possibly could.

I selected my rating, which was an 'Operations Specialist'. I was the guy in the search and rescue command center who would receive the "May day" calls and dispatch resources to their location. I would also learn to manage the computer system that would simulate if someone fell in the water in position 'X' and where they would be in 2, 4, 6, or 8 hours from now, giving our team the highest probability of success to find them.

Living in New England and being stationed in various parts for the past 16 years, I have run and managed some severe cases. I became extremely good at my job because I knew how important it was if someone needed the Coast Guard's help. However, not all severe cases had happy endings, and I have been the last person several mariners have talked to.

It takes a toll on you from time to time. You often ask yourself, "Did I do everything in my power to save these people?" My answer was always yes, because I tackled each case like my wife and kids were the ones I searched for. But too many things in this life are out of your control, and we have to learn how to develop the skills to manage that.

After a full decade of being enlisted, I felt I was ready for the next chapter in my life. I worked hard to put together an Officer Candidate School application package. I had to go through the interview process, bring certain test scores of mine up to become eligible, and gain a certain amount of college credit.

It was not an easy task for me, because I honestly slacked off so much in high school that college was brutal. I lacked a lot of key fundamentals that would help me as an adult. Regardless, my motivation and dedication to become an officer in the armed forces were high, and I wouldn't stop until I received an appointment to OCS.

I got the phone call one rainy afternoon in November from the recruiter who was helping me. She told me I was selected and would attend the class in January the following year.

I remember breaking down and crying, maybe the first time I had shed a tear in as long as I could remember. I am extremely passionate and emotional, but very rarely do I cry. I was with my son at the time, and he asked me, "Daddy what's wrong?" I told him, "Your life just got a whole lot better."

I loaded him up in the truck, and drove to my wife's work. At the time, she was an assistant teacher in the local school. It was almost time for school to get out, so I waited in the parking lot right next to her car. I could see her and my daughter walking to the car, and I tried to compile the words to say.

What ended up happening was that I just jumped out of the car and yelled at the top of my lungs, " I did it! I got selected for OCS!"

They both ran to me, and we all hugged as a family. It was a very special moment. We then drove to both of my wife's parents' houses and told them the good news together. We also called my parents and extended family, too, and let them know. Everyone went out to dinner that night to celebrate.

As much as I wanted to be an officer for the job, a substantial financial benefit followed. Up to this point, we were mostly a single-income family. When we had our first child, we lived in Portland, Maine, and only had one car. I would walk to work from our little apartment in the dead of winter.

On the weekends, I would referee wrestling matches to make additional money. We had enough money to give our kids everything they wanted and needed, but, as a result, my wife and I would eat ramen noodles or Hamburger Helper at night. We struggled hard for the first several years in our familyship.

Being young parents can go either way. You can ask your parents for help and money all the time, or you can work your ass off and try to prove to the world that you are capable of doing all of this on your own. My wife and I chose the work your ass off method. That is not to say that sometimes our parents would not help us, but it was not something we asked for or expected.

January of 2019 came, and I went off to OCS. This was a 17-week program that I had to go to, which was in resident training. This means no cell phones, no visits, and just getting your ass kicked morning, noon, and night on top of the most challenging academics I had ever experienced.

I put my head down, worked hard, and received my number one pick out of there, which got me back to Boston so that my family did not have to move.

Graduation came, and my whole family from California was in attendance. When I say whole family, I mean just about everyone. Parents, sister, grandparents, aunts & uncles, cousins, the whole nine yards. We had a huge party and celebrated my success. It felt absolutely amazing to have that kind of support, and I am so grateful for my close family. I was now a military officer!

I would commute to Boston every morning at four-thirty for the next three years. I was the Sector Boston Deputy Enforcement Chief, leading a team of six to conduct High Interest Vessel Security boardings. We would go way offshore, and my team and I would climb up the sixty-plus-foot Jacobs ladder, onto an eight-hundred-foot ship, and go through it with a fine-tooth comb to ensure compliance with all federal laws and regulations.

I felt so a part of something. We had such a great team with so much experience. It made me feel like I was competing again with a sports team. We worked out, ate, and slept in the same barracks room. I still had a family, though, and I still had youth sports. Which meant I still needed to be a good husband and father.

I would spend hours in the car driving to and from work, to and from practices, and to and from games. I put nearly seventy thousand miles on my car in two years! I felt like I lived in my car.

I had to learn how to manage workplace stress, come home and forget about it, and be a good father and husband. I struggled with this a lot. My work phone would always ring, and I would have to step out of games to take calls from my superior officers. Playing the juggling act was real.

Someone asked me once, "Cody, how are you doing?" I said, "I am just trying to juggle a few more things than I think I can right now, and it's getting close." He told me that life is all about juggling things. Some balls are glass, and some are rubber—just don't drop the glass ones. I really took that comment to heart, and I try to live by it to this day.

Everything we do is a balancing act; when we take on new responsibilities, we have to let go of others. I often say that I wish there were more hours in the day. I could use about a thirty-hour day to accomplish everything I need. But that isn't the case, and that is never going to happen, so I need to prioritize my day and objectives so that I do not drop any of the glass balls in my life.

* * *

After COVID happened, and our kids went through remote learning, my wife and I decided to homeschool them. I should specify that when I say that 'we' home schooled them, I really mean that my wife home schooled them.

She is an extremely smart person—the type who can just look at something and eventually figure it out. At this point, their math was already getting too difficult for me, and I just had to fall into a support role. Luckily, I can be quite a good cheerleader when I need to be.

Anyway, we are now a home school family, which comes at a price. So many of our friends have said, "I can't believe you have the patience to do that, be with your kids day in and day out." It was hard for my wife to hear that. Our kids are our life, and I can confidently say that we have raised some pretty damn good humans because I absolutely love hanging out with my kids. Another comment we would get is that they are not getting enough social interaction, with the added question asking if we are worried they might turn out a bit weird. My wife would always reply, "Have you never met a person who went to public school and was weird?"

At the end of the day, our kids never stopped doing sports, so they were with a team (and other kids) almost five days a week, getting plenty of social interaction.

This is to say that, as a result of homeschooling, our kids' education actually flourished. Yes, my wife is an amazing teacher, but the learning environment was different, too. The distractions were those you created in your own home, instead of distractions like little Jonny making a huge stink in class and causing everyone to wait while the teacher addressed the problem.

In our home environment, my wife could let them work for twenty minutes and then go outside for fresh air. They took several field trips and did their class work out on the beach or at a park. It was honestly such an amazing experience for us and our kids. We even bought a Mercedes Sprinter van and decked it out and took some really awesome road trips.

After doing this for a couple of years, we started to think about what we would do for the rest of their educational journey. We knew that several of our friends sent their kids to Catholic school.

My wife and I are both religious, not over the top. I like to say that I believe there is a god, and I know that god is not me (to quote Rudy). So, we gave it a shot and went and toured the local Catholic school.

We quickly fell in love with the structure, uniforms, and environment where all the parents had the same vested interest in their kids' success. After submitting applications, both of our kids were accepted.

As I write this, they have been going there for a few years. Of course, we still deal with problems—it is not an end-all, be-all that just fixes everything. But the environment is good, allowing a ton of confidence to flourish in our kids.

At this point in the story, I am an officer, our kids go to private school, and we have a pretty expensive house. I make good money, but I am not rolling it in, and times have gotten a little tough. We are no longer saving anything—cutting a check for almost twenty thousand dollars for your kids to go to school was, and still is, extremely hard for us. On top of the nearly four-thousand-dollar hockey tuition, guitar lessons, swimming lessons, the list just goes on.

We needed more money, plain and simple.

I have always tried to figure out what to do with my life once I retire from the Coast Guard. I wanted to own my own business, but I didn't necessarily know what I wanted that business to be. So, I kept searching for what I could do for a bit of a side hustle.

One of my friends owns an extremely successful painting business, which sparked my interest. This also all came up around the time that my wife wanted our house painted. I assured my wife that I could do it.

Naturally, I watched a bunch of YouTube videos and immediately thought I was a professional painter. Kidding, I knew I was far from it, but I went and bought a cheap airless paint sprayer and a very big ladder, which was a great first step.

I took a few days off work , and I painted the entire house in mid-August. It turned out great , and my wife and I were very happy. The previous owner kept meticulous records of everything he and his wife did to the house, so I saw the price they paid when they had it painted. I noted that the price I did it for was about fifteen times less.

I asked my wife what she thought of me reaching out to a few people in our community to let them know that if they needed their house painted, I could do it. I knew that with a few jobs, it could be the end of our means regarding school and sports tuition. My wife was actually dabbling in real estate at this time, and had a client who needed their basement floors painted.

Well, the rest is history.

I started a business. I registered my name, "Cody Seevers Painting," with the town, got insurance, and started building my inventory with painting equipment. I also began to have a ton of fun learning how to run a business. I would charge much less than my competitors, which landed me a lot of jobs. In addition to my competitive pricing, people loved the idea that I am active duty in the Coast Guard, and still busting my ass after work to help our family get ahead in life.

I worked like a madman for a year and a half, and by the time it was nearing its end, I had hired a part-time employee and was working sixteen-hour days between the Coast Guard and painting. Though exciting, this was taking a toll on me; my body, attitude, and so many other things. My wife had to pull me aside and have a serious conversation with me. She told me that she and the kids barely see me and that I fall asleep on the couch mid-conversation with her. It was not okay. How long could I continue to do this before it really took a toll on my body?

My wife and I decided that when I became a Lieutenant, the salary increase would make up for the loss of the painting income, so I could walk away from that and be more present. Thankfully, I made Lieutenant a few months after that conversation and phased out of painting.

Having the painting business taught me so much, including the most invaluable financial lesson. It was the golden handcuffs effect: You are making great money, your family is doing great, and everyone is set up for success. But you are a prisoner to your work, which is being prioritized.

It is important to note that everyone defines wealth differently. Most look at it in a literal sense and associate it with the number in their bank account, or what all of their assets are worth. I define it as my family and my health, the roof over our head, the food on the table, and the fact that we all love each other unconditionally.

As I think most men feel, I want to protect, provide, and preside (I learned that from a podcast called "Order of Man"). 'Provide' is the one that is most associated with money. We want to make as much money as possible to ensure our family is cared for. This comes with a sacrifice to our mind, body, and spirit. Finding the balance between making enough money to give your kids opportunities and spending quality time with them that they need to develop and become great people is challenging.

Just remember, you only have one life and one shot at being a good parent to your children. If you feel you are neglecting your duties as a husband or a father, just pause, look in the mirror, evaluate what is going on in your life, and see if small adjustments can be made to improve your relationship with your family.

I have found that if I prioritize my wife and kids, my overall happiness is much higher than if I prioritize money. When you take on additional responsibilities, you must also sacrifice current responsibilities. If the responsibilities you neglect fall to your wife, she will have to inherit additional responsibilities around the house.

The most important thing about all of this? Communication. Don't ever stop talking. Find the common ground, agree to disagree, but move in the direction of family first, and money second.

I am not telling you to live beyond your means. I am just saying to ask yourself if what you are buying is a need or a want. If it is a want, then put it on the back burner. I know my kids are more happy to spend time with me than they are to get that new hockey stick or a new guitar. Being a strong father figure to your kids will make this world a better place, and strengthen you and your wife's relationship.

I am still not perfect with this, and I struggle daily with prioritizing what I want and need. The self-awareness factor comes into play here; if you know you struggle with it, at least you can work on it. Admitting you have a problem is the first step!

> *There are two types of players: the interested player and the committed player. The interested player loves the game and, when they come home, puts their bag next to the door. The next practice, they grab the bag and go. The committed player, on the other hand, brings their bag to the basement after practice. On off days, they work on taking shots, stick handling, watching their favorite NHL team on TV, and maybe even doing some conditioning to better prepare themselves for the next practice or game.*
> *You can't want it more than them.*
> —Coach Paul

CHAPTER EIGHT

Always Follow the Coach, Not the Organization

In New England, our school breaks are different from those where I was raised in Southern California. Here we have February vacation, which is a week off from school that allows families to escape the mayhem, go to a warmer climate, and replenish their Vitamin D.

I am not kidding, when you live out here for an extended period, people will talk to you about the winter blues. Over the past several years, I have come up with a running joke called "March Madness." This means when the March Madness college basketball tournament is on, I know I am almost through the madness of winter, and can start looking forward to spending some time out on Sandy Neck with Friday night beach bonfires and a few wobbly pops.

During February vacation, my family tries to go somewhere to get a little bit of that feeling early. Get some sun and recharge the batteries. In 2022, we went on a cruise to the Bahamas. It was absolutely amazing, just me, my wife, and the kids. We let them stay up way too late and do just about anything they wanted. It was almost like a modified "yes day". I was so happy to just put work, school, and sports to the side and think about nothing but my family.

But, as always, there's no real escape from it.

The way that cruise ship meals are set up is that you sign up for a certain time slot and are assigned seating with another family. My wife and I are always hesitant about this because you never know what wack-job you are about to share a meal with. However, this time was different. We sat down with a family that had kids the exact same age as our kids and parents who were only a bit older than us.

We started off the conversation with basic small talk about where we were from. Lo and behold, they were from Massachusetts as well, about two hours away from us. We laughed at the coincidence, and I asked the man what he did for a living, to which he replied he was a Police Officer. I chuckled a little and said that I was kind of like a water cop in the Coast Guard.

Amid a relatively normal conversation, things got real.

I made the mistake of asking if their kids played any sports. What do you think their response was? Yes, of course, their two sons played hockey in the FED league (which is considered the highest competitive youth hockey league in Massachusetts). I told him that my son played as well, and then we proceeded to talk about hockey for the next hour and a half—along with the next three nights.

The dad was a really smart guy, and I could tell that he has experienced what I am going through—not only as a player himself but also as a father raising two young men.

His kids were extremely well-behaved and polite; you could tell they were a good family. I asked him if the leagues they played in were as political as the league my son played in (Boston Hockey League), and he assured me that all youth hockey is political—no matter if you are on a town team or a club team. Somehow, some way, it is always political.

What he told me next really changed my perspective on how I view hockey (and youth sports) in general. He told me that what league the kids play for and the players on the team don't matter, but what matters most is the coach teaching your child the game and helping them become better people.

You spend roughly seventy-five percent more time practicing than you do competing, and during that seventy-five percent of time, all the development happens. Kids are able to take risks without any consequences. They can try that cross-over as hard as they want, and if they fall, it's okay.

There are two types of practice players: the player who wants to be the fastest and the player who wants to master the skill at hand. Being the fastest will, without a doubt, get you noticed during youth sports. However, the player who focuses on the fundamentals, and maybe falls a few more times because they are trying to get it down to a science (the way that it should be done), has the potential to not peak as early as the one who rushed through it.

He made it very clear to me that how practices are run is arguably the most critical piece to the puzzle in your kids' advancement throughout the various levels of competitive youth sports. I have never and will never forget that.

He also proceeded to tell me that club hockey is ruining town hockey. I asked him what he meant by that. He told me that, in his day, there were no club sports. There were only town sports. Not only that, but all the players took pride in playing for their town. As a result, it was extremely competitive. As time passed, one organization would essentially create a "super" team to play in tournaments, and the evolution of club teams exploded. Others began to recognize these tournament teams and would follow suit, cherry-picking the best of the best from the town teams, putting them into tournaments, and traveling all over, stacking up wins.

It is similar to what we see in professional sports right now—the team with the highest salary cap that is able to manage its finances and attract the best players has a substantially better chance of success than those who do not.

As a result of this leaking into youth sports, a league would pop up, and the creation of club teams began. This took some really good talent from towns while leaving them with a lot less revenue coming in.

If we were to compare and contrast some of the best club teams to town teams, there are such large differences. The number one difference is the cost. I would venture to say that the average cost for any club hockey team in the Northeast is upwards of four thousand dollars. Some of these do not even take into account uniforms. This also does not account for travel expenses, hotels, food, and swag (you always wind up getting your kid a sweatshirt or something at all the tournaments for the first couple of years, then you realize they have ten of them and cut that off real quick).

Town teams are roughly half of that total cost.

The real win is if you find a town team that also owns an ice rink. These are the hidden gems in youth hockey. Since they are a town-run and operated organization, they will typically have a much more advantageous practice schedule that is more age-appropriate and more accommodating with practice time. Also, because they own their own rink, the coach can scoop up empty sheets of ice at no additional cost. What I am getting at is that town teams with a rink have the potential to see the ice much more, and at a much lower price.

When I put it like that, it seems like the decision on which type of team is better for your child is obvious. However, the argument persists because it remains a numbers game. If they have too many kids for any one age division, they will create "A" and "B" teams.

Chances are, a dad (or several dads) who had a high school hockey career at best will be your kid's coach, not a trained professional. The town will also never turn away a kid who wants to play hockey, so if your town only has one team due to numbers, the chances of a kid being on your team who has never skated before is a real possibility. On the other hand, if they get the numbers and have two or more teams, this is when the most bang for your buck can really happen. It is a chance that you have to decide if you are willing to take.

Oftentimes, kids who play on a club team will also play as an alternate for their associated town. If the club team only offers practice two days a week but your child would like to skate more often with little to no commitment, the town will gladly take your money, and they can be an alternate.

It is usually half the tuition price, so let's just say one thousand dollars at most, and (if the practice times coincide with your club team) you could easily find your kid on the ice seven days a week. At the age I'm discussing (8-10 years old), that might be a bit much. However, the option is there if you and your child are comfortable with them putting in the extra work.

Overall, one of the reasons club/ travel youth sports teams have such success (and therefore remain the choice for many families) is because they can target an audience from a larger area. For example, if there is a hockey club out of Rockland, MA, they can take on kids from pretty much all of Boston, South Shore , The Cape, and even towns heading west. When you compare this to town teams, you will only find an overlap of players if the town the player lives in does not have a team and travels a few miles to the next town to get involved in that program.

Like I mentioned previously, people associate club hockey with wins. They feel that paying all this money should come with wins. However, that is not always the case. There is such a high level of competition in youth sports that you really have to work your ass off to stay in the top tier.

However, as kids get older, club teams fall apart. Kids move from one team to another because parents are constantly trying to get their kids on the best team possible. Sometimes, this can work if their child is talented; other times, it can really play a significant role in the kid's development. For example, you never want to get "labeled" as the parents who pull your kid and go from one club to the next every single year because nothing is good enough for your child.

Something else to consider is that once your child gets to high school, the club season is cut in half so the kids can play for their high school.

I personally find it really rewarding that this is still happening. There is nothing better than playing sports for your high school. You get to experience playing with the same group of kids for four years straight. Playing town sports all the way through can give you a head start on this. That way, come time to play high school, you already know your teammates. It makes for a great cohesion of players and a whole lot more fun.

* * *

Regardless of the type of team you are on, being on the ice more than five days a week and not getting into bed until nine or even ten o'clock at night is not allowing these kids the adequate rest they need for proper brain function. It takes so much coordination and energy for meals, homework, and just being a kid. It is often way more than the kid can handle, and that is why you have such a high burnout rate in high school or the years following.

We (parents) are causing this. We are pushing our kids past their ability, and sometimes, I have seen a child's development go backward. You really have to have serious conversations with your family about the level of commitment you are at and the duration of the season to make sure you are making a well-informed decision. Additionally, your child should have a say in this, as they are going to be the ones putting in the work.

The point that I am trying to make in this chapter is that no matter where you decide to play, the only thing that matters is the coach and how they fit with your family! It's clear that no matter where you choose to play, there are countless variables beyond your control. But one thing you can choose is your coach.

Point blank.

You could be a part of one of the best club teams with a coach that is a complete asshole, and your kid could shut down and no longer perform. You could be on a town team with a rockstar coach who knows kids and how to manage a practice, and your kid could have a breakout season.

When you look into a program, club, or town, you should ask who the coach is and if you can meet with him or her. Whatever organization you are playing for should afford you that opportunity. At this point in time, regardless of your kid's ability, there should be a conversation between you and the coach to determine if they are the right fit for your child. There is nothing worse than choosing that club team because there was so much excitement, and getting a quarter of the way through the season, only to find out that the coach you were promised is not the coach you got, and the kids do not react well to their leadership and forget the basic fundamentals of the sport.

Choosing a youth sports program should be as simple as selecting the right painter for your house. Ask yourself, "Who do I feel the most comfortable with my kids being around?" and "Is this kind of person someone I could see myself drinking a beer with?" Maybe, "How does he treat his own child (if he or she has one), and how is the child's behavior?"

This is a big one—way too often, I have seen coaches with kids who are the absolute life of the party in the locker room. Whether the coach is good or not, they will always have a power struggle between separating from being their child's parent to being their coach, which is a challenging task to accomplish while trying to keep the best interests of the team in mind.

When choosing your coach, don't be afraid to be picky, and don't worry about how good the team will be. Worry about how good the coaching is going to be. Worry about how your child's hockey skills will develop and whether this coach will teach them to be a better person.

I once heard a parent say, "I'm trying to raise a gentleman, not an NHL player." If you remember what we covered previously in this book, the chances of making it to the professional leagues are very slim, and therefore, we should all be trying to put our kids into situations where we raise them to be better people than we are. If we continue with that mentality, we will create a better generation with hope.

Remember, "If you hang with dogs you get fleas."

CHAPTER NINE

Your Marriage

Before we dive deeper into youth sports, I want to share how my wife and I met—not just because it's meaningful to me, but because the strength of your marriage or partnership is the foundation for how you'll show up as a parent. Navigating youth sports requires unity, communication, and mutual respect. If that core relationship isn't strong, everything else—schedules, decisions, support—starts to unravel.

I have been married for 16 years to the world's most amazing and beautiful woman. How I tell the story of how we met is very different from how she tells it. I will tell you my way.

I had just joined the Coast Guard, and, after completing Basic Training, I received orders to a "Surf Station" In Chatham, Massachusetts. Being from California, I had no clue what Cape Cod was in my upbringing, and I had to Google it when I became aware of my new assignment.

It just so happened that one of my best friends, whom I had met in Boot Camp, also received orders to a cutter (Patrol Boat) out of Woods Hole, Massachusetts, so when we both had time off, we could see each other. Jay Bermudez is a great guy from New York, and he had a girlfriend who would come up to visit from time to time.

One day, the couple invited me to go to the movies with them. I really did not want to be the third wheel on their date, but she insisted that I go so I could meet her. I had nothing else to do, so I went along with it. They picked me up, and we drove in his yellow single-cab Dodge Ram (Hornet edition) to the good old Hyannis Movie Theater.

We found a parking spot, and I was just opening my door when this absolute smoke show whipped into the parking space next to me, almost taking my door off as she screeched into her spot. I quickly shut the door, avoiding the near collision. She made the cutest little smirk at me, and I smiled back. We exited the car, and my buddy, his girlfriend, and I walked into the movie theater.

We were standing in line to purchase tickets, and I noticed that the mystery girl was now sitting at a bench by herself near us. I thought there was no way she was waiting for just a friend, but she was probably waiting for her boyfriend. I kept glancing at her, which was obvious enough for my friend's girlfriend to notice and mention. She asked, "Are you just going to keep looking at her, or will you go over and talk to her?"

In the past, I have never had any issues going up to anyone and starting a conversation, especially girls. I loved talking to new people and meeting new people. However, for some reason, I was considerably more nervous this time around.

Jay's girlfriend said to me again, "Just go talk to her!" So I approached the mystery girl and asked, "Do you come here often?"

It was a horrible pickup line, but nonetheless, it got us started in a conversation. I discovered she was somehow not waiting for a boyfriend, but just one of her friends. The sigh of relief filled my veins knowing that there might be a chance to ask her on a date, but for whatever reason the next thing that came out of my mouth was that I was having a little party back at my apartment, and that if she and her friend wanted to stop by, they should. I also told her that I would give her my phone number and not ask for hers in case she never wanted to see me again.

The ball would be in her court.

I thought that was a clever idea, also putting a lot on me to think I was charming enough for her to ever call. Either way, that was my first interaction with Miss Blake Bridges of Sandwich, Massachusetts.

After our conversation, I went into the movie, but struggled to focus on anything except how beautiful she was and that she had such a profound aura around her. She was not like the other girls I have dated in the past. She seemed so mature for her age, with a presence that made everyone stop what they were doing and look when she walked into a room.

I was honestly in love with her from the moment I met her.

Later that night, while sitting in my apartment by myself—yes, I 100% lied, saying I was having a party to look cool—I got a random phone call from a local area code. The movie theatre mystery girl was on the other line with the most satisfying voice I have ever heard. She said that she and a few of her friends were out, and they would like to stop by my "party".

A million thoughts raced through my head; Could I quickly invite a few people over and tell them to say we were hanging out all night? That wouldn't work because I didn't have many friends at the time. So, instead, I proceeded to lie in my panic, and I told her that everyone had just left and it was much smaller than I expected. In addition, I had to be at work early the next morning and would most likely be going to bed.

I thought for sure I ruined my chances, but at least now I had her phone number. I woke up that next morning and had to use everything in my power to not text her just to say hi. If I remember correctly, I made it until around ten in the morning before texting her.

We began texting back-and-forth, which continued for about a month. During this time, we really got to know each other on a different level. We would ask generic questions such as, "How is your day going?" but we would often find ourselves in a really deep conversation.

I remember asking her to go out a few times, and we had a few dates planned, but she inevitably canceled on me at the last minute each time. One date I was particularly proud of was when I borrowed two jet skis from a friend I was stationed with. I planned for us to bring lunch and head out on the jet skis to a remote beach on Cape Cod for a picnic, while also exploring areas on the water that were inaccessible by boat or land.

To me, this was a top-notch date idea. Little did I know, just about that time, there was a huge case on the news about a man accused of killing his wife on a jet ski and dumping her body in the ocean. All of her friends told her that she did not know me well enough, and that she should not go if she wanted to stay alive.

We laugh and joke about this all the time now, but she canceled on me again that day, and I was devastated at the time. I thought, "What must I do to hang out with this girl?" I have put together some of the best ideas I can come up with, and still nothing.

So, we went quiet for a day or so, and then she reached out. "Would you like to go to the beach tomorrow?" she said. In my head, I wanted to respond, "Yes" as fast as possible, despite being canceled on several times before. But I practiced extreme patience and waited a few hours before answering, "Sure, I would love to, but chances are you will cancel on me again." Her reply keeps me chasing her to this day: "Take it or leave it."

Needless to say, I took it.

We went to a quaint little beach on North Shore Blvd. and parked the car. We got out and took a nice walk on the beach, picking up our conversation that originated over text messages.

We talked about life, big picture things; What we wanted to accomplish in the world, and who we wanted to become. We both had big dreams, and we shared all of them with each other on that date.

I remember that at one point, we started to feel really comfortable around each other, and I knew she had her bathing suit under her miniskirt and top. It was a hot summer day, and I would have done anything to try to see her in that bikini. I picked her up and waded out into the water, laughing and kidding with her that I was going to throw her in. "You are not going to throw me in," she said with a playful tone. So, hearing the dare in her voice, I gently plopped her in the water, surrounding us with the beautiful Cape Cod ocean on an absolutely gorgeous summer day. It was truly perfect, but the best part was that I was holding her in my arms, and I was unbelievably happy.

I remember it taking every inch of self-control not to try to lean in for a kiss at the end of that date. Instead, I thought of a way to show her that I was classy while still letting her know I was extremely into her. I leaned in, kissed her right on the forehead, and told her it was the best first date possible.

The rest is history.

We have hung out every single day for the past sixteen years, despite me being away on Military assignments and a few other stints when we had to work with a long-distance relationship.

We got to know each other on a level I have never known. We had difficult conversations early and often, talking about things such as whether we wanted kids and how many. She wanted to have four, and I wanted to have two, so we settled on three (for the record, we only have two, and from time to time, I hear from her that she wants to have another kid). We talked about how we would raise these (at the time) future kids. Did we believe in spanking them (her reply was absolutely not)? Did we believe in time-out or not? How good are we with our money? Do we have credit card debt? We talked about everything, and we aired out all of our dirty laundry early on. At the end of the day, it brought us so much closer, and we were extremely in love.

I knew she was the one after our first date. I called my mom and said, "Mom, I think I found the girl I am going to marry." Now, this came as a shock to my mom because I was the guy who told everyone that I was never going to get married and that I wasn't going to have kids—I just wanted to be a bachelor my whole life.

Maybe there was some truth to that, but deep down, I longed to find someone that I could put up on a pedestal, and look up to, and admire. In return, you hope that they think of you in the same manner, and if that is the case, constantly work to strengthen your relationship.

The first time my parents met Blake was in Arizona. Being a Southern California kid, we would go out to the Colorado River each year and ride jet skis, wakeboard, and water ski behind the boats. We would bring out our motorhome and stay for a long weekend, basking in the one-hundred-or-higher degree, dry, desert heat while emerging yourself in eighty-or-higher degree water and drinking beer all day long. It was an absolute blast.

The first time I went home on leave was a few weeks after my twenty-first birthday. I was home and hanging out with family and a few friends when my mom asked me what was wrong. I told her that I wished Blake had come out with me. She didn't skip a beat as she said, "Well, then fly her out; you still have a week left in your trip."

The next thing I knew, I had Blake on the phone and asked if she would come to California and spend the weekend with me if I booked her a flight right then and there. She said yes without hesitation. A few moments later, my credit card had a much larger balance than it did the day before.

A few of my buddies and my parents headed out to the river that morning, so the plan was for my sister to pick Blake up at the airport and drive her down since she was not planning to leave until later, too. I still laugh thinking about it—Blake, having just met my sister, stuck in the car the whole three hours down and getting interrogated like a father talking to his daughter's prom date. All out of big sisterly love for me, of course.

Nonetheless, Blake survived the ride and made it out to the river. I picked her up on the beach on my jet ski, and we took off on about an eight-mile ride up the river with majestic red mountains in the background. Once we reached our destination, which was a huge sandbar that everyone pulls their boats onto and parties all day long, I proceeded to spin the ski around in a 360-degree manner in hopes of tossing her off and getting into the water. To my surprise she stayed on. Later, my mom would tell me that she was watching from the sandbar, and that this is when she knew she was a keeper.

We made landfall and Blake met my entire family. My family is extremely welcoming, and it didn't hurt that they were all half crocked at this point in the day. We had an amazing weekend riding jet skis and exploring, and I was able to show her a true staple of my childhood.

I proposed to her after only five months of being together, and we got legally married the next month. She moved home from Keen State, which was about three and a half hours away, and started going to school at the local community college while working. We already had the wedding planned for July 24, 2009, but sometimes military members get legally married earlier for other reasons. We were one of those.

After we got married, we enjoyed our time together and were eager to start a family. Blake got pregnant a few months before I left for Operational Specialist "A" school. This was a five-month-long school in Petaluma, CA. During this time, Blake temporarily moved in with my parents to be in the same state as me (California). My parents would drive their truck and trailer up to where my training was for a week here and there, so I could hang out with Blake and them in the evenings and weekends. My grandparents would even take turns coming up and staying for a week at a time so that Blake and I could be together. Once I received my orders to Portland, Maine, Blake returned to Cape Cod with her family and began the quest to find us an apartment to live in for the next four years.

When I was finished with school and we moved to Maine, it was only a month later that our beautiful daughter, Aislynn Blake Seevers was born. She was the most amazing thing I could have ever asked for. If you ever question your faith, being a part of the childbirth process will solidify that there is a God.

Once Aislynn was born, it was just the three of us. We had help, but it was three and a half hours away. We were doing this on our own, which was the best thing for us as new parents. We got to make all the decisions without exterior recommendations.

It's not that our families were opinionated, but we got to make the rules the way we wanted to make them. We were confident in the way we structured our parenting style because, from early on, we had those tough conversations and aligned our values into one T.E.A.M—Together, Everyone, Achieves, More.

As a result, our parents respected what we were doing, and we were able to set healthy boundaries. A few years later, we had our second child, Ezra Cody Seevers, before I took another assignment down on the Cape. We were able to return to Blake's hometown and really start to dig our roots.

Now that you understand the foundation my wife and I built together, let's shift back to youth sports, because the way you parent through this journey is directly influenced by the strength of the partnership behind the scenes. If you do not agree on everything and cannot disagree on something productively, then whatever you are trying to accomplish will fail. Each person must give 100% effort. There is no relationship where you can get away with it being 70/30 yet still expect it to be long-lasting and happy.

Of course, there are times you will fail at this—I know I do. But you have to recognize when you are failing and make the effort to get back on track. You have to be able to call yourself out. If you don't, animosity will sink in, and you will never succeed as a couple.

* * *

Blake was also an athlete growing up, so sports are very important to her. When we entered the world of youth club sports, I don't think either of us knew what we were getting ourselves into. However, we agreed on what we were doing, and, therefore, we were in it together.

The phrase "it takes a village to raise a child" is all so true when it comes to sports and sports teams. There will be times when you need someone to pick your kid up and bring them to practice or when you are the one doing the extra driving. If you and your spouse are not on board with the investment you are making in your child's sports teams, you will not be successful.

My wife and I had to have a few long conversations over the years to ensure we stayed on the same page. For example, I was ready to commit to a team off Cape Cod with practice three days a week in the evenings and games on the weekend. She had to sit me down and explain that our nine-year-old doesn't need to have a fourteen-hour day three days a week, with more games on the weekend. She explained to me that if we did this despite the driving commitment, there is a strong possibility that he would get burnt out and no longer want to play hockey. After this, I realized that I was being over the top.

The point is, my wife and I made the decision together. It was not me telling her that this is the team he will play for. It was not a one-way conversation. I am sure it is like that for some of you, but if you want to have a happy wife (which makes for a happy and more pleasurable life) you cannot make these decisions without their commitment. Chances are, your spouse will have to do some pickups and drop-offs and help out, so failure is imminent if they are not on board.

Plus, a serious amount of politics surrounds the world of youth sports (with emphasis on youth club sports), and having your partner as another voice of reason is helpful. When you are paying top dollar and making those three-hour drives to games, the expectation is that all the kids should be performing to a certain level. If your kid is one of the kids that is not the star on the team you can hear unwelcomed comments in the stands about how little Jonny should have gotten that pass instead of your kid, or that your kid should have held it longer before dumping it in the offensive zone so that the play wasn't offsides.

These comments can be difficult if you are a passionate person.

With all our experience already, my wife and I are still having conversations about our son's future in hockey. I would be lying if I told you we were not thinking about going back to town hockey to make sure that he enjoys playing a sport that he loves with his friends while making good memories.

Lately, the coach for a town team and I have been communicating, and he offered my son to come play for his team as an alternate. We took him up on that offer and have gone to two games at this point. He had the best time and skated amazingly. He was able to position himself to contribute to a team that he had not played with for several years and make a difference immediately.

The atmosphere was great, and the parents were great. We had a great time in the stands just talking about our kids and how much fun they were having. This was a breath of fresh air to my wife and me because for the previous several years it had been such a different environment. I was grateful that we made this decision together for our son.

We have also been encouraging him to consider sports other than hockey. As a result, we signed him up for baseball this spring. I want him to have these opportunities so that when he looks back on his life as an old man, he says that he played "all sports" and has great memories with friends and his parents and sister coming to cheer him on.

This world we live in is so negative that it can really get the best of you if you are not in the right headspace. We need to do a better job as parents of finding joy in this world and having fun with every opportunity that we get while encouraging our kids to do the same.

CHAPTER TEN

Baseball

When my son was around five years old, we signed him up for tee-ball, just like thousands of parents do across America. In this league, and especially at this age, it is unreasonable to think that a single coach can wrangle up almost two dozen five-year-olds and have anything productive come out of it. Therefore, there were segments at practice where the coach asked the parents to help out with their son or daughter. I thought this was brilliant—what better way to help, spend time, and have fun with your kid without the full coaching commitment?

One day, during batting practice, the coach lined up several tees down the first base line, and all the parents and kids flocked to them. We were each handed a pile of balls to go with our tees, and there were some basic instructions given by the coach (prior to these kids thinking they were Babe Ruth and drilling one deep into center field). I don't know how much listening was going on, but you could visibly see the kids foaming at the mouth at the thought of swinging the bat with all of their might, just trying to make contact and send the ball as far as possible.

One after another, these kids teed up and just started ripping them. Some made contact, some missed completely, and others hit the tee and sent it flying. It soon became chaos, but I was laughing the entire time while keeping a sharp lookout for an accidental discharge of a bat that went flying.

Everything up to this point had been going fine, and we were having a pretty good time. Next, the coach told us to have the kids turn and start hitting with their non-dominant side. He continued to explain himself by saying there is no time like the present to learn how to be a switch hitter.

As much as I think it's a highly skilled thing to do (and it would be pretty cool for my son to be able to do that), I can't help but think that I don't even know if my son is going to stick with baseball. The kid is only five!

Hitting from his dominant side, my son was doing great and having a blast. Once he made the switch, he struggled a bit and quickly became annoyed. He told me he wanted to return to hitting the way that was working. I didn't skip a beat when I told him to turn back around and just have fun.

What I didn't realize was that he was the only kid who spun back around, and now it was very apparent that he was doing it the 'wrong way'. The coach approached us and told us that he needed to return to hitting it the other way.

I had to use every ounce of self-control not to tell this guy that he's nuts and that the kids just want to hit. I mean, at this point, they can't even catch. Why don't we work on that before we start teaching them how to be switch hitters? Instead of making the scene, I told my son to jump back around and give it his best shot to see how far he could hit one.

We made it through the practice, but the fact of the matter remains at large: aren't we supposed to be creating environments where kids can have fun and fall in love with a sport before teaching them a skill that is too far out of reach? As coaches, don't we need to teach age-appropriate skills to foster the greatest learning environment? Don't we need to ensure that it is fun to create retention in the programs? The answer is yes to all of those.

After that baseball season, my son didn't want to play again. I am pretty sure it was just too slow for him. However, I accomplished what I set out to do—I exposed my kids to all the sports during their childhood and found out what stuck.

* * *

A few years went by, and my son turned eight. At this time, we had the foster twins (a boy and a girl) living with us for just about a year. I wanted our foster son to experience all the different sports too, so I sat both my son and foster son down to talk about how cool it would be if they played baseball on the same team, and that I would even try to be the coach. I explained that we would have so much fun together, while encouraging them to say yes and give it a try.

They both agreed, so I quickly signed them up. My buddy at the time was pretty involved in the Little League community and also had a son my kid's age, so he offered to be the head coach, with me as the assistant.

As the season was fast approaching, I went out and bought a couple of baseball gloves, two helmets, and cleats, and had the boys try them on. They were stoked and talked about the upcoming season like they were in the big leagues. I took them outside and said we should throw the ball around a little to prepare for the season. I knew that my son knew how to catch with a glove, but I didn't know about my foster son at the time, so I figured we would start small and work our way back.

I taught him how to open and close the glove, when to turn the glove over to catch a lower ball, and when to leave the glove parallel to the ground to catch a faster chest-level ball. We were making good progress, and he was starting to understand the concept quite well.

However, I may have progressed through the steps a little too fast.

As we backed up in the yard, gaining more distance between us, I had to increase the speed of my throws. At release, I could tell one of my throws was going straight towards his face. He never moved his glove up to catch the ball, and it crashed right into his nose, causing an eruption of blood to come out. I ran over and held his nose, hugging him and apologizing repeatedly.

The kid was much tougher than I was at that age, because he cried for only a second and then told me it was not my fault and that his glove should have been up higher. This brought tears to my eyes because, in that moment, I realized that he handled the situation like a champ, and just like I had during a situation from my youth when I got hit in the face with the ball. If the adults in my situation had handled it a bit differently, maybe I would have stuck with baseball. Regardless, the kid was tough as nails, and after a good clean up we continued to play baseball in the back yard. This time with a softer ball, though.

The season ended up being great, and the kids had a lot of fun with my buddy and me as the coaches. We made sure we were always positive and truly let them be kids.

This was a coach pitch league, meaning we would lob balls at them until each kid got a hit. Sometimes, it was brutal, and kids would take double-digit pitches to connect with one, while others would rip one right off the bat. The score wasn't really kept, although the kids from both teams would tell their parents walking to the car that they won.

I always laughed because of how competitive kids are at that age (and really just in general). I am a firm believer that there is a winner and a loser in every game.

Teaching a kid how to lose is one of the greatest lessons one can learn over their life. We are not going to win at everything we do in life—we will not always get the promotion or have the highest sales numbers quarter after quarter. But what we do in the face of adversity can truly change the outcome of our lives.

For that reason, there should always be a winner and a loser. Either way, after that season of baseball, my son again told me that the game was just too slow for him and that he didn't want to play, so we went back to the hockey rink.

* * *

As I hinted at earlier, I, too, had an experience in my youth that ultimately made me walk away from the sport of baseball. To this day, I am still bitter about it because I think I could have turned out to be a pretty decent baseball player. Instead, I allowed one bad experience to persuade me that I did not like the sport.

I was eight years old, and I was a member of the Detroit Tigers Little League Team. Getting a uniform that looked just like the one the men in the MLB wore made me so excited to jump into the season. Some of the other kids had played the sport before, but for me, this was uncharted waters. I quickly caught up to my peers with basic skills (such as catching, throwing, and hitting).

This specific season was well on its way, and we had not won a single game. We all felt pretty down because playing the game isn't always fun, but winning is almost always fun. It did not help that our coach was pretty hard on us.

I was playing second base when a well-hit ground ball was pointed right in my direction. I shuffled to the left and moved my glove into position. Right when I was in direct line with the ball, it took a monstrous bounce off what I believe to be a rock or pebble in the field, and continued on a collision course with my face. No matter the age or the toughness of anyone, this hurts, and I don't think anyone would argue that with me. I instantly started to cry as blood poured out of my nose. With only a few more innings left in the game, I made my way to the dugout and decided I would not return.

After another loss, we circled up in the outfield, and our coach told us everything we did wrong. It was almost as if he would take notes in the game and, without saying names, would call out several people who may or may not have "lost" the game for us. On this day, he said, "We need to make sure we move up on the ball and are more aggressive so that we don't take one off the face."

Even at eight, I knew he was speaking directly to me. I also knew he was probably right by saying this could have possibly been avoided by coming up on the ball and not allowing it to come to you. However, that was the last thing I wanted to hear.

At that moment, eight year old Cody grew a big pair of balls and blurted out, "Well if you would make baseball more fun, maybe kids would want to come back and play for you next year." What I was basically doing in that situation was telling him that I thought he was a dick, he made the game not fun, and I would not be coming back to play next year. I don't even remember what he said following my comments, and, to be quite honest, it didn't matter. I was done. That single moment changed my opinion on baseball forever.

Or did it?

As a parent (or a coach), we have to teach, react, and adapt our style for age appropriate behavior. Just like in the example at the beginning of this chapter, where we explored whether we really need to teach kids how to switch hit at the age of 5? Similarly, if a kid takes one off the face, do we need to tell them that if their glove was there, that would not have happened?

Timing is everything, and much like in adult life, it is not what you say but how you say it. We need to communicate with kids using age-appropriate intentions behind our words; this goes for parents, coaches, or both. Of course, a parent carries the most influence, simply because you're around your child far more than their coach is. By consistently demonstrating the behavior you want to see in them, you'll see results faster and hold yourself accountable to act and carry yourself in the best possible way.

* * *

Fast forward to January of last year, my son is nine years old and will turn ten in March. I recently just engaged him again about what sport he will do once hockey season ends. In the past years, he typically went right into lacrosse. Lacrosse is one of the best parallel sports to hockey. They both require sticks, passing to the open sections in the field, there is hitting, the comparison list goes on and on. He also loved it and was pretty good at it.

For some reason, he had some hesitation when I asked him if he was going to do lacrosse this year. He asked me what other options were out there. I told him he could try baseball again and explained they would be the ones pitching to the batter at this age. I also mentioned that there would be a catcher.

When I said catcher, it sparked an interest. He started asking me a few questions about the positions and what not. One of my friends from work is super into baseball, and his son plays catcher. So, I shot him a text and asked him his thoughts. He told me that he had an extra set of catcher's gear, and that I should come grab it, throw it on him, and throw a few baseballs at him in the basement to see how he likes it.

I told Ezra I had a big surprise for him when he got home from school—he had no idea I went and picked up all this gear. When I showed it to him, he had a sparkle in his eye that told me he was all in. He probably didn't even care about playing baseball; he just wanted to put the gear on and see how cool he looked. I don't blame him—I was the exact same way when I was his age, so I played right into his excitement. I helped him put one piece of gear on at a time, and, by the time he was all strapped up, he looked like a stud. He was so pumped.

We went into the basement and just started playing catch. I wanted him to get used to catching the ball again in a glove, and this time, it was a catcher's mitt, which is quite a bit different than an infielder's glove. He picked it up quickly, and wanted to assume the catcher's position.

We reviewed the proper technique, and he jumped right into catcher mode. I started throwing him some strikes, and he thought it was great. I figured this would be a good time to talk to him about what happens if he gets hit with the ball. I wanted him to gain confidence in the gear he wore so that he knew he was protected.

I had him stand up and stood about two feet away from him. I told him that I was going to bounce a ball off of his face mask so that he could experience what it would look and feel like. He laughed and thought it was funny, so I took a few little tosses at him. I then moved to his chest and allowed the pads to do their job, all while reassuring him that he was protected. We then moved to his shin pads, and I did the same thing. Eventually, we both felt more comfortable, so I took a few steps back and said I was going to do it again, but this time a little harder.

I continued our routine, throwing a couple more off his mask, chest, and shins, allowing him to build some confidence with his protective gear. My reasoning was that if I threw a wild pitch and the first time he took one off the face, he wasn't expecting it and got scared, I'd traumatize him and he might not want to play catcher anymore. My plan worked, and he laughed as I bounced baseballs off various parts of his pads. With the confidence that his pads would protect him, he flourished in that position and soon, he would be hearing the crack of the ball enter the glove with force as a result of a hard pitch and a good catch.

As time went on, we started laughing and joking more. He even started saying funny things to the nonexistent batter. We reenacted the whole scene from The Sandlot talking about how if he had a sister as ugly as his dog then he would shave its butt and teach it to walk backwards. At this point, my son was almost rolling around on the floor and I had tears in my eyes from laughing so hard. In those forty-five minutes we had really bonded while working through the fears that lay ahead of playing a sport that he has not played in a few years. I threw one last pitch, and we ended with the crisp sound of the ball hitting the sweet spot in the glove.

The next day, he came to me and said, "Dad, do you want to throw some pitches to me?" It had worked; he was hooked, and I was excited for his enjoyment of a new chapter in his life. So, without hesitation, I agreed, and down to the basement we went.

Although this time, after he took several catches to my pitches, I asked him if he wanted to throw me a few strikes while I played catcher. See, I knew he had a good arm based on how he was throwing the ball back to me from being in the catcher's position. I felt that he could really flourish as a pitcher.

He agreed and took off all his gear while we discussed the various pitching wind ups. He settled on one, and the next thing I knew, he was laying down straight heat to me. I was thoroughly impressed that he was so accurate with hardly any focus. He was just throwing fast to me and playing catch. I told him that he was doing such a good job, that he should be proud of himself, and that he should be open to whatever position is needed for the team when the time comes.

Over a two-day period, he went from having no interest in the sport to walking around the house with a baseball glove and a rubber ball, throwing it up and down and bouncing it off the walls while catching the grounders it spit back at him.

Kids at this age are a product of the environment they are surrounded by. This is the textbook result of 'how a parent reacts to a situation will dictate how the child reacts to the same situation.' You see it now on Instagram, a parent with a very young child will tap the wall with their hand and act as if they got hurt and fake cry. The result is that the child will start to cry because they know no difference, and they are mirroring the outcome that they just saw. Then, you see the same parent change their face to a happy, positive face, and the kid immediately stops crying.

I have seen parental overreactions again and again on various levels of parenting and coaching. If a kid falls down (and it is not too intense), just sit there for a second and tell them they're okay. The actions will most likely result in the kids not panicking. The opposite example is if the kid falls down and you run over and say, "Poor baby, are you okay?" The kid will go into a tail spin and probably start to cry.

How you approach the situation will ultimately dictate the outcome of the child's reaction. Now, what I am NOT saying is that if your kid does something that is serious, you should just sit there and say, "You are okay." You have to know your time and place. If it is a little slip, trip, and fall and you know your child is not seriously hurt, try a cool, calm, and collective approach and see what the outcome is. I bet you will be surprised.

CHAPTER ELEVEN

The Interview – Billy Laninovich

Earlier in the book I mentioned one of my best friends growing up, Kenny. He and his brother Billy both had big impacts on my life for different reasons. Billy is one of two individuals from my hometown who, quote-on-quote, "Made it Big" as a professional athlete. He signed a big contract with various motorcycle manufacturers at the factory racing level.

I felt that it could add value to interview him about the things that he experienced growing up in the youth sports world, such as his relationship with his father, who was pushing him for success, in addition to other good life lessons that he has learned through his career. I know so many people have looked up to Billy personally and professionally for a long time. I want to gain perspective on the process that he took to become a professional athlete.

So, without further ado, here is our conversation:

* * *

Cody: So tell me, who are you as a person without mentioning a motorcycle?

Billy: I am a Christian, husband, uncle, brother, and son.

Cody: Do you feel that professional athletes are born with the God-given talent, or is it something that hard work and determination can overcome?

Billy: I think a combination of grit and God-given talent is where professional Supercross/Motorcross racers come from. Too many times, I have seen really promising new talent working their way up in the amateur circuit with tons of hard work and determination. Still, their talent is just not there, so they stay amateur while others go to the professional level.

Cody: When was the point in your amateur career that you knew you could make a career out of riding a motorcycle?

Billy: Growing up, my neighbor and I would ride our motorcycles together almost daily for three or four hours. I remember being around fourteen years old and saying to him, "I'm going to race Supercross some day." He laughed at me.

I was extremely motivated at this time and started to travel around the United States to compete at a higher level. I just loved everything about it. I honestly just loved riding my motorcycle; therefore, practicing was just icing on the cake. My mom would load up the Chevy Suburban with the tow-behind trailer and take me riding everyday if I wanted to. So that is what we did.

At fifteen, I started getting support from Yamaha, and that year, I took 4th place at Loretta Lynn's National Race. Following that, Yamaha gave me a free motorcycle. It was really at this point that I realized that if a motorcycle manufacturer believed in me, I knew I had what it took to get to the next level.

The following year, I went out and won my first National!

Cody: How do you define success as an amateur athlete?

Billy: I think racing motorcycles is unique in different ways, including how you measure success. For example, if a C-class rider goes out and competes at a national-level race and gets a top 10 finish, that would be a successful race. However, if someone who has been to these national races and has competed at an extremely high level for a few years goes out there and gets 10th place, it would be a failure. Defining success in racing and action sports generally differs from conventional team sports.

That is one of the reasons I love this sport so dearly. If I went out and gave it my absolute best effort and, as a result, finished the race on top of the podium, I could be proud of myself for a successful race. On the flip side, if I went out and put in my best effort, but just maybe wasn't feeling it that day, and perhaps barely broke the top ten, I could only be mad at myself. This sport is a very self-giving and self-taking sport. At the end of the day, success in racing and action sports is defined by winning. When you get into the professional ranks and are a part of a factory racing team, it is your job to go out and deliver results.

Also, priorities can change at any point in the year. I have always valued staying healthy as a part of success. This sport is so intense and dangerous, but if you want to be able to compete for an overall championship, you have to be in the races to win the races. If you are on the sidelines, you have no chance of winning. Therefore, success can also come back from an injury and build back up into race shape by displaying slow progression upon your return.

Cody: What is the hardest step in going from the amateur level to the professional ranks?

Billy: In the amateur racing scene, you would always have the top five guys who were really fast. When you transition from amateur to the professional stage, all twenty or forty guys, depending on whether you are racing Supercross or Motorcross, are the best motorcycle racers in the world. That is a mental hurdle that takes some getting used to. Just knowing that there are so many different riders with the speed to win makes it all the more difficult.

Also, when you are an amateur, the style of tracks is different. Amateurs do not (or at least not when I was coming up) have unrestricted access to the best Supercross training tracks around. Practicing on a Supercross track is a whole different beast than racing on a Supercross track. When you turn professional, you find yourself on a Supercross track multiple times a week. There is a huge adjustment period, not only for your mental state but also for the sheer physical ability, to handle these obstacles on a repetitive basis, and continue to build upon your success day in and day out.

Then, put all of that aside, you are training all week long, flying to the races on the weekends, racing, and then flying back home to start training again. You spend a lot of time in hotels and living out of a suitcase. These are all things that require adjustments. Being able to adapt quickly is a really good thing.

Cody: Do you believe parents (specifically dads) could ruin a career before it even starts?

Billy: 100%, parents can burn a kid out. I have seen it time and time again. I have witnessed dads out on the track yelling at their kids and telling them to jump this big jump that is way out of their skill level. I understand they are trying to push their kid, but what they're asking for is beyond the child's current abilities. They haven't developed the bike control needed to make the jump they're being told to do. Then, if this continues, and the kid keeps getting hurt, there will come a time when the kid just wants nothing to do with it anymore.

The parents can't want it more than the kid wants it. At the end of the day, you have to love what you are doing. You will never reach the next level if you are not passionate about it.

I have also seen it unfold where these kids have nothing to lean on when they finally decide they are all done racing, because they are so burnt out. The parents do not support it. Oftentimes, in these cases, they start hanging out with the wrong crowd and drinking alcohol, maybe even getting into drugs. Physiologically speaking, it can be very damaging.

Cody: How hard did your parents push you?

Billy: I would say that my dad didn't push me too hard up until the point in time when I started winning on a bigger stage. This was probably around the time I was sixteen and had won my first title in the "B" class. Looking back on it now, though, he never pushed me too hard to the point that I wanted nothing to do with it. I think he saw that I had what it takes and was trying to mentally prepare me for the next chapter in my professional career.

Being a professional Motorcross racer is so different from conventional team sports. You do not have teammates around you when coming up through the ranks. Your team consists of the individuals that you surround yourself with. And often, my dad had to push me out of my comfort zone to get me ready for the next level. My mom was always in the support role—someone I could talk to after a good or bad race. She has always believed in me, and I was able to experience the best of both worlds with my parents.

I remember this one time we were at the World Minis and I was expected to compete and do really well at this race. I was signed up for four classes to race in, I wound up winning three out of the four. I remember my dad being mad that I didn't go four-for-four.

I think that is when I realized that the expectation to win was the priority, no matter the cost.

Sometimes, you need someone to be hard on you, though.

When you are young and do not have all the life experience your parents have, you need to lean on them for guidance. Everything happens so quickly when you are this age. I started winning big races, getting free motorcycles, riding daily, and working hard. Then, I had the personal side of life, where I still loved hanging out with friends, and started hanging out with girls. My dad was there to ensure I never lost focus on the end result. I would say it was very age-appropriate, and it never got to a point where I was pushed too hard.

Cody: If you were to go back and tell the nine, twelve, or fourteen-year-old Billy Laninovich words of advice, what would you tell yourself?

Billy: Have fun with it! I just really loved riding my dirtbike. Any professional athlete has to absolutely love what they are doing because there comes a point when it is no longer a hobby that brings you just straight happiness; it becomes a job. I was very fortunate that I was able to have a job that happened to be the thing I loved most in life.

There are so many ups and downs—battling injuries, sickness, and personal distractions—that you really need to remember that this all started because you loved doing something so much that you put all of your effort into it and became one of the select few who can call themselves a professional athlete. Enjoy every second of that because it can all be over at the drop of a hat.

There is no difference between racing motorcycles and working in the corporate industry when you are on a factory racing team. You are expected to show up to work, do your absolute best, and make money for the company. If you are not doing your job, there is always someone else that is willing and able to put in the work and take your spot. There is no room on any professional sports team where you are just there to collect a paycheck; you have to earn it.

* * *

Billy's career highlights include.

- 2-time Monster Energy AMA Supercross Championship 125WSX 4th place (2005, 2003)
- 2006 Monster Energy AMA Supercross Championship SX Lites W 5th place
- 1 career Monster Energy AMA Supercross Championship 250SX West win
- 8 Career Monster Energy AMA Supercross Championship 250 SX West Podiums competing in the X Games Best
- Whip competition

Most recently, Billy set his sights on coming out of retirement at the age of 40 to see if his skills could be tested against the best in the world. This is a true testament to the burning desire within professional athletes who truly love what they do to the core.

In 2024, after not racing professional Supercross for over a decade, his return left him in the record books.

His successful qualification into the main event etches his name in the history books as the oldest racer to have ever made a main event.

* * *

I genuinely enjoyed conducting this interview—it was filled with meaningful takeaways. I especially appreciated the chance to reflect on the unique differences between team sports and action sports. For example, Billy defines success as a racer as winning. If you recall, in our first interview, Nick defined success as continuing to grow and sticking to a process to be successful in your sport. This difference explains the true difference between these two types of sports.

Billy's passion for his sport also stood out to me during this interview. To work your way up all the various stages in sports, you have to have the passion to push through on the days you don't want to get out of bed. This undoubted passion is also seen now, with Billy returning to racing after a decade and making history as a 40+ year old going against guys more than half his age. All the while, he is grateful for the opportunity to continue to do what he loves.

We as parents cannot teach our children passion as it relates to sports. It is a self-made feeling. They will either love what they are doing or they will not. Exposing your children to all different sports, music, acting, dancing, or fishing—it really doesn't matter what—but exposure to everything gives our children the opportunity to find out what they are truly passionate about in this world, and can give them joy and happiness for the rest of their lives.

CHAPTER TWELVE

Basketball

In 2024, I had the pleasure of being the head coach for my daughter's seventh and eighth grade basketball teams. I say pleasure because it really gave me the opportunity to spend more time with my daughter, and get to know her social circle better . What I didn't realize was that coaching young women is much more difficult than I imagined, and totally different from coaching boys.

I assume this could be a controversial topic of discussion, but at the end of the day, these are my feelings and opinions. There is a distinct difference in the way you coach girls vs. boys. This can take a while to learn and/ or recognize, but there is a big difference, no matter how you view it.

I had heard that girls can be easier to coach because they tend to be better listeners and more polite than boys. After my experience, I can agree and disagree on this. I would show up for practice early and well prepared to run an efficient practice. Sometimes, during warmups and stretching, it sounded like the gym was filled with fans because of the sheer loud volume that was coming from them.

I had to figure out very fast what type of coach I was going to be. Was I going to take the drill instructor approach and have law and order, or would I take the more laid-back approach and let them have fun?

Early on in the season, after getting frustrated several times by the noise in the gym and all the side conversations about "girl things," I knew I had to have a discussion with all of them. I will never forget this conversation because I think it was the moment that we came together as a team for the first time. I had them all sit down on the bleachers and told them that I would wake up for work at six in the morning, work straight through without taking a lunch break, and leave work early to drive forty minutes so that I arrive on time to their practices and games. All while being well prepared with a solid practice or game plan with a starting lineup.

I told them that if I was putting in this much effort, then my expectations were that they would match me so that we could work together as a team and make progress.

I also asked them what their expectations were for the season. I think this is extremely important for a coach to ask. What if all of the girls you are coaching couldn't care less about basketball, and they just want to have fun with their friends and play the game? If that is the case, and you are taking the drill instructor approach, it will not work out.

In my scenario, I am talking about a middle school girls' basketball team. I had twelve girls show up for the team, and we took all twelve; there was no cutting a player because they had never played before. So, these are things that you have to know and understand as a coach. If you are coaching an all-star team, the expectation will be slightly different because there was more of a process involved that led your players to be there. In my case, I had no clue what the expectations were, so I asked.

I asked them to take some time to think it over and discuss it as a team before getting back to me. If their goal was simply to have fun, be with friends, and ensure equal playing time, we could do that. But if they wanted to compete and aim for the Super Six Championship at the end of the season, I was also ready to push and motivate them toward that goal. What mattered most was that our expectations—coach and players—were aligned.

I let them talk amongst themselves for a few minutes before walking back over and saying, "Well, have you girls reached an agreement?" They had, and they wanted to compete. I made it clear to them that if they want to compete, then that is what we would do, and I confirmed that I wouldn't ask anything of them that I wouldn't do myself.

Right then, I told them to get on the line—we would start the practice running sprints. I blew the whistle, and they quickly moved their bodies to the line. Only this time, the side conversations were a little bit less.

To their disbelief, I lined up with them. I guess they did not know how literal my statement of 'I won't ask you to do anything I wouldn't do myself' actually was.

When the whistle blew, I took off and sprinted as fast as I could. I went down and back, crossing the blue line first. I wanted to set the standard for what a winning mentality looks like. I saw girls running, but not to their full potential. I let them know that we were going to run sprints until everyone displayed one hundred percent effort. I blew the whistle again, and we all took off. Again, I was the first across the line. I am not that fast, but I gave it everything I had.

I still didn't see the effort from the group I sought. I started raising my voice (not in a bad way, but in the way that slowly builds) with each sprint that we did. Each time we returned to the line after a sprint I pulled something motivating out of my ass while adding volume. I once told them that, compared to them, I'm an old man and out of shape, but we'll keep going until everyone gives 100% effort. I even raised the stakes by saying someone has to beat me before we stop.

My plan was to show them that, even with me huffing and puffing, I would sprint and work hard every whistle, because that is what it takes to compete. As my motivation and excitement grew, I noticed first that no sidebar conversations were taking place, and second, they were determined to beat me. At this point, they were actually right on my heels, and I knew they would get me in the next few sprints. Still, I didn't give up; I wanted at least one of them to beat me fair and square.

A couple of sprints later, I wasn't the first to cross the line—I blew the whistle and made a really big deal out of the girl who beat me. While clapping, I explained to her that that is what it is all about. All the other girls, as exhausted as they were, joined in. In these twenty minutes (that felt like hours), I had accomplished two things: I knew their expectations for the season and led by example when running the sprints with them to show them that I was as equally invested in this as they were.

It was our first team victory.

Through the season, I made our lineup and associated playing time not based on skill but on the effort I saw during practice. I wanted to incentivize hard work, with the reward being that they got to play more in the game.

* * *

Being the coach of my daughter's team was very difficult. A coach's child gets either one of two scenarios—they play way more than anyone else, or they get screwed out of playing time because the coach (their parent) doesn't want other parents to think they are favoring their kid.

I battled this all season long regarding her playing time. Some weeks, she played a lot, and others, she played less. If I stuck to the effort equals playing time rule I created early on, I was able to write down my top five effort producers each week, and it made the decision easier for me.

Halfway through the season, my number two point guard showed signs of putting all the work, effort, and skill together. All of a sudden, she looked very comfortable with the ball in her hand, dribbling down the court.

I will never forget this one play for as long as I am alive. We were in a neck-and-neck battle with only a minute left in the game. She was showing a 'never give up' approach. I had her jump into another position she was not used to playing, and she didn't even bat an eye. She was well prepared and paid great attention during practice.

I had her and the full-time point guard take the ball down the court together, passing it back and forth in an attempt to confuse the other team. Once they got to the top of the key, they broke out and drove in for a layup. Our plan was successful, and we tied the game and found ourselves in overtime for the first time that season.

I had a really solid plan for four quarters, but I was not prepared for overtime. I made a few changes to the line up, and they went out there and had a back-and-forth battle, each team scoring on each possession. With thirty seconds left in the game, I called a timeout.

I brought the girls over and had the whiteboard on full display. Our starting point guard scored a lot of points in the beginning and middle of the game, but, just like any good team would do in the later minutes of the game, they started to double-team her, and as a result, we stopped moving the ball and having scoring opportunities.

My plan was simple: Inbound the ball, and take it down court to get it to point guard number two. See, I knew she had a good shot. She had been working extremely hard at practice, and, at this point in time, I wanted her to have the ball in her hand when the final buzzer sounded.

The ball came into play, and it was a full-court press. They did everything possible to keep the ball out of their defensive zone. We made a couple of quick moves and entered scoring territory. With nine seconds left, the pass was made. I could see everything slow down. I had wanted this so badly for her, knowing she had it in her. She marked up to the backboard and took a jump shot right outside the key. As it hit the backboard, I knew there was no chance it was missing.

The crowd went wild when the ball finally passed through the net. The score put us ahead by two, and the buzzer sounded. Our team flooded the court, along with all the parents in the stands. It was such an amazing feeling as a coach to watch something like this unfold. I was so happy for her success.

CHAPTER THIRTEEN

Psychologically Speaking

Whether you know it or not, psychology is in every part of life. In the modern era, you have seen the utilization of sports psychologists increase drastically. Virtually every college, national, or professional sports team has a paid sports psychologist on staff.

If you were to ask one hundred people what percentage of sports is mental, you'd probably get one hundred different answers. I would make an educated guess by saying people would say that sports are between 50–90% mental.

I don't have an exact number that I would place on the mental aspect of sports because I think it can vary depending on the sport. If I were to give a ballpark, it would be somewhere between 80-90% mental. I believe I chose the high end of this because once you have put in the time and effort and proven to be amazing at what you do, the only thing left is to go out and do it again and again.

Physically speaking, you know you can do it, but now, mentally, you have to back this up.

Here is the best example I can think of: why is 'golf' a four-letter word? All the other four-letter words were taken. At the professional level in golf, they try to hit the ball in the hole in the fewest strokes possible. However, whenever a professional golfer steps up to the tee box at a par three, they do not expect to get a hole-in-one. Moreover, they plan to put themselves in a position to have a great second shot. I would venture to say that every professional golfer has gotten a hole-in-one once in their lifetime, but that doesn't mean they do it every day, week, or month. It is something that rarely happens despite knowing that it is possible. It's because, mentally speaking, it's not possible. Physically speaking, you know it can be done.

Here's the thing, though: no matter what percentage, mental toughness is undeniably a crucial factor in sports. It's universally understood to play a significant role in performance. Whether it's staying focused under pressure, pushing through fatigue, or bouncing back from mistakes, the mental aspect can be just as important as physical skill. In fact, it's almost always agreed that the answer is never "Sports are 0% mental"—no one doubts that mental toughness is essential in sports.

But what does that really mean, and how does it work?

That's what I wanted to explore. So, I decided to dig into sports psychology to better understand how mental strength impacts athletes and where this concept even comes from. Are there specific cognitive strategies that make a difference? How do top athletes develop resilience? Why is this information important to parents of youth athletes? These are just a few of the questions I set out to answer.

I met with one of my great friends, Dr. Jay Toomey, who happens to be a licensed clinical psychologist. Jay also has kids around my kids' age. He is an all-around great guy who has actually coached his girls on various sports teams.

We ordered a pizza, grabbed a case of Guinness, and sat down to talk about psychology as it relates to youth sports and parenting in general.

Here is our conversation.

* * *

Cody: What is the difference in how moms treat their sons compared to their daughters? And how do fathers treat their sons differently from their daughters?

Jay: If you were to just talk to people, there is a general understanding that mothers are harder on their daughters, and fathers are harder on their sons. Dads dote on their daughters while mothers coddle their sons. However, there is really no great research that supports this claim. In reality, parents tend to parent their kids based on their individual needs and personality. Parenting styles also vary depending on the parents that the adult experienced.

As someone who has two daughters, I can see that I can treat my daughters differently from time to time based on their very different personalities. One is goofy and outgoing and is into dance and things like that, while my other daughter is more into sports and academics.

Cody: What makes a healthy relationship between anyone?

Jay: The most important thing in a relationship, whether it is a romantic relationship or a parent and a child, is trust. Trust comes from experience and witnessing that person acting in a reliable and predictable way. Those are also two major characteristics people look for in someone they want to have a long relationship with. They ask themselves, "Is there a level of predictability with this person when I need them to be there?" They look for the sense that when that person is with them, they are not putting on a show or an act and are willing to be open and vulnerable.

This all goes back to the trust that you have built with this person.

Emotional stability is also crucial in a relationship. You need to be able to maintain equilibrium.

Cody: In my house, we have a rule that if you come to us (the parents) and tell us if you did something wrong, you will not get in trouble. No privileges will be lost, we will talk about it and move on. What are your thoughts on this approach to parenting?

Jay: It is essential to establish with your kids the understanding that they can come to you when they have done something wrong and you won't get mad; instead, you will listen openly. This is important in a parent-child relationship because it signals to the child that your love for them is not contingent on them doing something or being a certain way. They can do something wrong, and you are still going to be there, and you are still going to love them.

When your kid does something wrong, they tend to overestimate how you will react because they have a very basic understanding of right from wrong. They get in trouble for doing bad things, and don't get in trouble if they do the right things. If they kick a soccer ball and break a window, and they come to tell you, then this will not change how you feel about them. It is not going to alter their guarantee of safety in this relationship.

This is by far one of the most important things you can signal to your child.

Cody: How many hours a day or week is too much for sports?

Jay: You won't get a good number from anyone on that. I think you really need to know your child, and you need to know the signals that they send. Depending on your relationship with your child, they may just be able to say, "This is too much for me." They may also signal it in a really obvious way, like this one, because they trust you will understand.

If they have concerns about the parameters around the relationship, in the sense that if you have signaled to them that your care for them and your guarantee of safety for them is contingent on them continuing to do a certain thing, they may hide things from you. They may hide the fact that they have reached their breaking point, that they are exhausted, or that they are hurt. They might think you will remove that care and love by either expressing disappointment, giving them the cold shoulder, giving them the silent treatment, or full-on lying into them for quitting or giving up.

Common sense is important. If your kid is out for 3-4 hours a night playing sports and is just going straight to their room without talking with you, they are signaling to you that they are exhausted and might be tucking something away. At this point, you should really try to speak with them about this. Ensure that you haven't accidentally signaled to them that they can't talk to you about this, or take a break—that is the most important thing.

There are a lot of misconceptions that if you check in and love on your kid too much, they will become a "Mamma's boy," or a "Daddy's girl." There is actually a lot of research on folks who are constantly showing love and affection to their kids vs others who do not, and the research shows that the more you hug and kiss your kids, the more successful and balanced they will be. Your kids becoming "Momma's boys" or "Daddy's girls" happens when your sheltering of them, your coddling of them, and your loving of them, is driven by your own anxiety that you then pass on to them. This is a likely path to have anxious kids who are too attached to and dependent on you.

But the love itself? It is impossible to love your kids too much. I think sometimes people are worried that if they love on their children and check in on them too much, it is going to make them "soft" when, in reality, it is quite the opposite.

Cody: How important is nutrition as it relates to healthy development?

Jay: Nutrition is very important for both physical and mental health. There is a lot of research on the negative emotions and psychological effects on overeating and intaking too much sugar and how both affect attention and mood. With kids, you can see this very easily.

There is also a great deal of research on how nutrition affects intelligence and basic cognitive functions. On the extreme side, malnourished kids can show significant increases in intelligence when you add protein and micronutrients to their diet. More typically, any parent can relate that when kids are hungry, their moods change dramatically. They may know that they are hungry, but they don't make the connection between their hunger and their mood. Very often, if your kid is acting moody and you feed them a healthy snack, it could fix the problem instantly. From a longer-term, developmental perspective, there is a reason why governments spend a lot of money and time on school programs to feed hungry kids and to make sure schools have healthy food options.

Malnutrition can be insidious in that a child can appear "well-fed" and still be malnourished because they are eating highly processed foods that are not nutritious. Unfortunately, for many folks, the choice is between feeding your kid highly processed foods, or not feeding them at all. In those circumstances, a little bit of homework can take them a long way.

Picking up a cheap multi-vitamin and then trying to ensure that your child is getting a good amount of protein, along with fruits and veggies, will take care of most nutritional needs.

Cody: What are some of the worst things you can say to your kids as a parent as they are growing up? (Even if you didn't mean it to be bad.)

Jay: The biggest part of the equation is not what you say to your kid, but how you say it, and what may be implied in what you say. For most kids, the most devastating message they can receive is that your love, care, and safety assurances are contingent upon them acting a certain way or meeting certain expectations.

I don't think any reasonable person would say to their kid that if they do not clean their room, they will no longer love them. But you may say one thing to your kid, yet what they hear is completely different. It could be that if they don't get good grades, don't make the soccer team, or don't score a goal, they might feel a lack of care or love. There's a fear that failing in these areas could result in not receiving the same support or affection. This is something that, as a parent, you need to be cautious of.

You need to be careful of what you project on your child. You do not want to put your own anxiety or your own baggage on to your kid. These can be current stressors, like stress at work or marriage, and they can also be your own personal regrets. You must teach lessons from your past because you have experience and wisdom related to this topic. However, it is also important that you do not give them the impression that Dad or Mom has certain expectations based on their achievements. You don't want them to feel that they're less worthy of love and care if they're not as good at something. On the flip side, they shouldn't feel that being good at something would make them more deserving of that love.

Cody: What are some of the most positive things you can say to your child for growth?

Jay: The words themselves are not as important as their message. The message you want to convey to your kids, especially those who are athletes, is that their experiences are meaningful regardless of the outcome.

What is most important is the lessons they are learning, not how many trophies they collect, or how many games they win. What gets a lot of kids to stay with sports is that part of the fun is winning, and it is less fun to lose.

There is still value in loss, though. There is still value in failure. What you say to your child in these situations could be a million different things, so long as the message is not, "It's because you aren't good enough." Or just shutting down and not saying anything to them.

I have seen coaches walk away after a tough loss and not say anything. At this point, you are withdrawing your support from them, and this message speaks for itself. In reality, after a hard loss is the most important time to teach a life lesson. What you say in these moments is less important than the overall message that failures are a part of life and important learning experiences.

The opposite is equally important when they are successful. You want to convey is that their success is because of their hard work and effort, not for some reason that they should take for granted. What you shouldn't say to your kid, and what you should say to your kid have a million manifestations, but the underlying message is extremely important.

Cody: Should we look at failure differently? Should we maybe even consider it as a building block for future success?

Jay: I find that kids rarely learn from massive failure. If they go out in a game and lose ten to nothing, there is typically not much you will take away from this, or the takeaway will be very obvious. I think kids and adults learn the most when they can see that they were right there. There is almost an excitement there, like if they did that one thing just a little better or faster, they would have succeeded. Thinking like this is what is going to take you to the next level.

Here is an example from my daughter's recent soccer tournament: They blew the doors off the competition all weekend and won the championship. However, she played defense, and the ball was hardly ever around her. She was pretty much standing around the entire weekend. She did not feel fulfilled. They won the championship, yet she did not feel fulfilled.

She expressed to me that they had lost games where she felt better. Or where there was a close win that she felt better. You learn a lot from close competitive games. You learn a lot about yourself and about your team. You typically do not learn much from huge blowouts.

This is why it is so important to ensure your child is playing at the appropriate skill and age level. When you are a contributing member of a sports team, you have more opportunities to gain experience and have successes that come with neuropsychological rewards, like a dopamine hit. These experiences train your brain to seek similar experiences that might require you to continue competing and improving. You may rob your child of that opportunity if you push them too fast and they end up sitting on the bench on the next skill level. Playing on a team of appropriate skill level is so much more impactful.

Cody: Do you think it is important to play multiple sports, or should you just focus on one?

Jay: Interesting question. Growing up, I played both soccer and basketball. There were things that I learned in soccer that transferred over to basketball and vice versa. Doing multiple sports also allows you the opportunity to exercise different muscles by engaging in different types of movement that would train other muscles, making you a much more well-rounded and physical athlete. So, I think there is that side of it.

I know different physical therapists who will talk about the maintenance part of it as well. Folks who tend to play multiple sports tend to be less injury prone—so I'm told. They may be training more supportive muscles while putting stress on different ligaments or joints to make them stronger and more resistant to injury.

The mental stimulation side of it is really important as well. Learning the strategy of different sports expands your cognitive capacities, which you can carry over from sport to sport. Typically, in basketball, you learn to play a pick-and-roll, which is illegal in soccer—you can't actually set picks per se—but the concepts can help you identify your position on the field. This is why I say there is also a cognitive component that helps you be more creative.

I also think playing multiple sports is beneficial from a social perspective. You will meet more people, and have more memories to look back on and reflect upon in life.

On a more professional level, being involved in several sports allows you to learn how to deal with conflict and adversity. I don't think anyone likes conflict, but most uncomfortable conversations you have to deal with come from some sort of conflict. Something has been done that is inconsistent with your expectations or values, and that introduces some sort of conflict moment where you are trying to win someone over and get someone to act differently or believe something different. Your expectation is that they are going to be confrontational towards you.

Having a background of physical competition gives you a platform of resilience in those moments. It often allows you to have less anxiety because you are used to dealing with challenging and difficult situations. That doesn't mean everyone who has played sports is better at having those conversations, because sometimes they simply don't have the knowledge base to support their position. But generally speaking, having a background in competition, especially in really challenging situations, like being in a "dogfight" where you have to stand up for yourself or risk being pushed over, can be beneficial. That prepares people for these types of conversations. They have less anxiety about these types of conversations because they have overcome that adversity on the field or the ice.

I don't want to overstate it and say that sports make you invincible, but they do give you the advantage over someone who has not experienced any adversity or has not had the experience of playing sports.

I try to teach my kids that all of life is 'school'. They tend to only think of 'school' as the place you go, but it is more than that. You learn lessons across all of life, and you use those lessons to advise you and to direct you later on—just like the stuff you learn in science class in high school will help you in science class in college, and if you become a scientist then it will have helped you in that job, and so on. All the things that you learn outside of school are learning experiences and opportunities to inform your life or behavior later on.

Cody: What are some good things that we as parents can do to self-check ourselves and make sure we are keeping on track with how we are handling things?

Jay: I think having a good support system around you, such as family and friends, is extremely important for various positive outcomes. For example, connect with other parents on your child's team—check in with them, see how they're doing, and how their kids are doing too. Having these conversations can give you an enormous amount of insight into how they are managing various situations.

There may be parents whose kids you can very easily see are struggling, and you can tell what is going on there. This is educational because it shows you that strategy does not seem to be working. And therefore, that is probably something that you are not going to try out.

It also gives you a chance to share some of your wisdom and help someone else.

But for those whose kids are doing well and having fun, their parents are also people you should check in with and ask what seems to be working for them. You know, something like, "Lisa out there really seems to be having a good time, and my kids seem to be struggling. What are you doing differently?"

There is a humility factor associated with this, though. It takes a good deal of humility to go to another dad or mom and say, "I really respect the way that you are raising your kid."

You also have to be able to not get down on yourself to think that you are doing a bad job of raising your kid. None of us are perfect, and we will not always know why our kids are struggling. Remember that why our kid is struggling will not always be our fault. But we can still gain valuable insights from someone else who thinks differently, has different experiences, and can help guide us along the way. We are not born with all of this wisdom; we have had to figure it out along the way.

Most likely, you have figured things out by watching someone else or being told by someone else. I think we rob ourselves by not taking the opportunity to get some of this wisdom and knowledge from someone else. I think, subconsciously, we are worried that this would signal to another parent that we are not as good of a parent as the person we are seeking guidance from.

We also need to check in with our kids and have regular conversations with them about these kinds of things. Parents often miss the opportunity to simply ask their kid if what they are doing as a parent is working.

Trust me, they will tell you if it's not.

We have to ask them what feels like too much. Whether they need a break or not is a huge part of it.

Cody: I have heard through conversations, "They don't raise them like they used to." I take this comment to mean that my generation and older were raised quite a bit differently than my kids are today. Tough love might be the better way to put it. What are your thoughts on this?

Jay: I think that if what people are talking about is that more recent generations coddle their kids too much, and that tough love is the way to go, then that is mostly bull shit. The whole idea that "They don't make them or raise them like they used to" can be very harmful. There is not a lot of great evidence that supports the idea that kids fifty years ago were better off emotionally or psychologically than they are right now.

That being a relative statement, I mean the last few years have definitely been a challenging time for kids. We have seen a massive increase in depression, suicide, and anxiety post-pandemic. This is a historical artifact though, and I do not believe it is an indicator of a generational approach to parenting, but more so a blip on the radar because a virus entered the world and caused a whole lot of havoc.

Prior to that, if we look back to the 1960s and 1970s (with the hippy generation taking over during this time), the older generation was saying, "Oh my god, they are ruining our country." Yet, following that, we had some of the most successful years in our history when those "hippies" grew up.

That is not to say they were better than their parents; it is just saying that their parents sounded the alarm too soon. It's also important to acknowledge that when new generations come along, they come into a society that is different from the one that the generation before was raised in.

Technology is different, the availability of information has changed, nutrition has changed—all kinds of things have changed. It is not necessarily something different about the person, but more about them adapting to the space. Their adaptation to the space looks different then the generation that raised them. I think if space never changed, then there may be some merit to that. At this point, you would have definitive proof that tough love "did work" vs. present-day parenting.

However, when the environment in which you are raised changes, sometimes the parenting techniques of the past become less effective.

For example, our kids have always known an environment where social media exists. They have literally always known a world where you could just get information at the tip of your fingers. I still remember having to go to the library to get an encyclopedia to get information to learn about Roman history for a class that I was taking. The other day, I witnessed my daughter asking Alexa for the answers to her homework—and getting them in seconds. Our generation would fight against that and say, "Oh no, no, you are not supposed to do that, that's cheating." But we now have all his information at our fingertips, so why not? It almost doesn't make sense to memorize certain types of information; you are using up cognitive resources that could be used on other things. That said, I think technology may be evolving a little too fast for us as a species, but the changes help to explain why things are so different.

Cody: What is your opinion on social media?

Jay: I feel like social media is like firearms that come with a bump of cocaine.
Right?
Firearms are one of the greatest inventions in human history. We wouldn't be where we are as a species without firearms. They have helped win the conflict between "good and evil," improving our ability to feed and protect ourselves. But they have also caused a tremendous amount of harm. Firearm deaths are one of the leading causes of death in this country. But you can't imagine society being where it is today without them.

So, there is a similarity where social media has fundamentally altered society in some very positive ways. It has connected us in a way that no other form of technology has. I can instantly communicate with someone on the other side of the world in a way that is more engaging or satisfying than sending a text message or email. I can get information quicker from social media.

But here is where the cocaine comes in—it's wildly addictive.

I can get gratification from it in a way that virtually nothing else can give me so quickly and so instantly because of the algorithms that they use. You enter a space where people immediately agree with you on topics. People who share the same ideas that you have. If you share something and they like it, that's a dopamine hit. You are chasing those likes and those little heart emojis and comments. The more of those you see, the more you are going to engage in that platform.

It is a very carefully crafted platform to foster engagement because engagement means money. These social media platforms have spent billions of dollars creating these algorithms to get people to engage in and get hooked on the space. The same way the cartels spend billions of dollars cultivating opioids and drugs and dispersing them to the population.

Not to sound too dramatic, but I think social media as an enterprise is pretty evil. I don't think they truly care about people; I think they just care about engagement and money. One of the best ways that they have figured out how to get people engaged is to flood newsfeeds with content that scares them and pisses them off. Because fear and anger are extremely potent mechanisms for engagement.

On another level, the platforms often create an impossible set of expectations for people. Think for a second about the things that people most commonly post. Are you likely to post the ugly or mundane side of your life, or are you most likely to post the best sides of your life? So, all you are posting is the best parts of your life and never the arguments that you are having or the absolute mess that your house is in because your kids haven't cleaned their rooms in forever.

The images that you are posting, even if they are not filtered, are ordinarily the best parts of your life which creates this constant pull to participate in the "keeping up with the Jones" circus. People are engaged in the comparison of life.

You constantly compare yourself to others—like when someone is going on a trip this year or adding a pool to their home—and it makes you feel envious and anxious. You start to worry that you're not on the same level as others in your category. When in reality, those folks are still experiencing the same stresses and the same downs that you are—you are just only seeing the positives.

There has been a lot of research on folks that engage in social media, and someone in that social comparison is far more likely to be anxious and depressed than the folks that engage in social media strictly from the stance of communication, such as keeping in contact with distant family members.

Cody: How do you define success in a young athlete?

Jay: The way that I define success for a young athlete is that the athlete is simultaneously having fun and improving. To me, that is all you want. The kid is having a good time and getting better at it. You are rarely going to find a time when the kid is getting better at something but not having fun with it.

Cody: How do you define success as an adult?

Jay: Kind of the same way, to be honest. I know my personal goal is to do something hard every day. Sometimes that is physically hard. A lot of the time, I can accomplish this by going to the gym and challenging myself to do one more set or one more rep than I did the previous day. Sometimes I can do it at work by accomplishing something very challenging.

I do this because as long as I do something hard, I have room to improve. When everything is easy, there is nowhere to go.

To me, being in a space where you constantly have the ability to grow is a great environment for success, particularly when you are enjoying yourself and what you are doing is consistent with your values.

Cody, you and I talked about this the other day when we had breakfast. The only lasting happiness is living a fulfilling life that is consistent with your values. All other happiness is fleeting or momentary. True lasting happiness is when you are constantly challenged and engaged in a way that is consistent with your values. So, to me, that is what success is.

CHAPTER FOURTEEN

Final Remarks

Every kid who has ever been involved in youth sports in some way, shape, or form has stood outside in their backyard with a ball in their hand or a puck on their stick. They closed their eyes and dreamed of it being game seven of the World Series with the bases loaded and two outs in the bottom of the ninth inning. Or game seven in the Stanley Cup, tied up and going to a shootout for all the glory.

However, as children grow, there is an inherent disconnect between the very moment they dream of and the reality of life. What is in front of them is so unknown. It is a very beautiful yet scary position to be in.

If I had the opportunity to go back and live it all over again, I would take it in a second (as long as I end up right back where I am in life right now). Childhood and adolescence in general are among the greatest gifts in the world, and yet when you are in the moment of it, all you can think about is being older.

So many people say that they have no regrets in life. That is a bold statement to make. Everyone should have regrets in their life. Nobody is perfect, and we have all made several mistakes. I think saying I have no regrets in life shows no weakness in the present moment, but is ignorant for the duration of your life.

I know for a fact that I would have taken school so much more seriously. I would have been more involved in things that I thought at the time were dorky, or that maybe the popular kids weren't doing. Who you were in grade school and high school is not the person you are when you are a grown adult with a spouse and children.

At every stage in life, you have the ability to change who you are. Just because you used to be someone does not mean you have to be that person for the rest of your life. Change is constantly around us. Sometimes, it's too fast for me if I'm being honest. However, change is how the world has worked for millions of years, and it will continue to change whether we are a part of this world or not. The more I think about it, as a father and husband, the more I realize that I need to focus on changing the things that will make a difference right now.

Do the things that will make your kids happy. Play catch with them for 5 minutes after work. Shoot pucks in the basement a couple of times a week. These moments that we have with our kids are only going to last so long, and then they are out of the house and set free into this world to do as they please.

A very wise Master Chief of the Coast Guard told me that I should always have a plan so that I never have to make a decision.

I love that saying for so many different reasons.

You can try to plan your kids' lives out to the fullest extent, and then one day they can wake up and say I'm all done with this and want nothing to do with it. Make your plan for the shortcomings, not the long haul, concerning your kids' futures. Let them be the ones who guide the ship in the direction that they want. Be there to help correct the course if they ask for it or if you see them struggling. Show your children that you are a good role model to look up to.

*　*　*

We have a serious problem with youth sports right now in America, and I can tell you it has nothing to do with the kids. It has everything to do with us as parents. We need to sit back and wait for the right time to push and challenge our kids, and I can tell you that before they are teenagers is way too early. During the teenage years, you can start to apply a little pressure while still making sure you never take it to an unhealthy level.

Then when they (or if they) decide to continue sports after high school, you need to go back to a support role. You want your kids to be able to talk to you about anything and share what they are feeling and dealing with so that you can be a part of the solution, not the problem. I know for a fact that if my kids ever tell me they don't want to play sports again, I would be crushed.

But I could live with it.

You know what I could never live with? My kids telling me later in life, around a campfire with their kids there, that they quit sports because I pushed them too hard and made it not fun anymore. That would be a complete failure on my part.

I want my kids to explain to my grandchildren someday that I was a man of balance. One who was all in and matched the level of commitment that I saw looking back at me. I was a man who led by example, and raised two damn good humans who went on to be successful in whatever career field they chose to do. Who taught two young men and women how to be loving spouses and devoted parents.

My life goal is to raise kids who turn out better than I did. If that happens, then I would consider this life that I've lived to be a successful one.

What else are we here for on this planet? Honestly, have you ever asked yourself why you are here? I have many times, and I don't know the answer. The only thing I think of is that I was here to meet my wife and raise our kids. To help empower those around me to be better tomorrow than they were today. Do more right than wrong. Say sorry when I make a mistake. Be a good person.

We need this today more than ever.

Remember this; your kids will love you no matter what. There is no right or wrong way to parent, so long as you are trying your absolute hardest.

When you notice you are slacking, you pick it back up again. You love unconditionally and teach them all the best qualities that you possess. If you mess up, say sorry, learn from it, and move on.

When you take your child home from the hospital, there is no owner's manual or instructions for you to read and know exactly what to do. There are books, blogs, and all sorts of other advice out there. But that all requires you to take the step and educate yourself on what you should or should not be doing as a parent. Take the pieces that work for you, and you will figure it all out on your own.

I hope you took something from this book and are able to apply it to your life right now. We have the ability to be the change that we expect, so please make some small changes and see how big the outcome will be.

God bless America and God bless youth sports.

EPILOGUE

After all the early mornings, late-night drives, and countless sacrifices, I've come to realize one thing—youth sports should never define us. They should enhance our children's lives, not consume them. They should teach valuable life skills, not create stress that lingers long after the game is over.

I've had the privilege of speaking with professional athletes, psychologists, and countless parents while writing this book. What I've learned is that the pressures we feel are real, but they don't have to be inevitable. We have the power to reshape the way we approach youth sports—to prioritize our kids' well-being over wins, to choose balance over burnout, and to remind ourselves that the journey is more important than the destination.

So, as you close this book, I leave you with this: Don't lose sight of what truly matters. Your child is more than an athlete. Your family is more than a sports schedule. And at the end of the day, no trophy or scholarship is worth sacrificing the joy of watching your child simply play the game they love.

Let's change the culture of youth sports—together.

DEDICATION

As I close this book up, I want to say a special thank you to my wife, Blake. She has undoubtedly been the solid rock in my life for the past 16 years. We have been through many ups and downs, and she has never given up on me, nor have I given up on her. She pushes me to be the best version of myself day in and day out. Sometimes I get annoyed beyond belief. Other times, I accept her criticism as a gift and try to make minor adjustments to what I am doing so that we improve our relationship. She has been the most incredible mother I could have ever

asked for my children. The relationship that she has built with them both is unfathomable. She is everything I could have ever hoped for or dreamed of.

I want to say thank you to my parents for raising me the way that they did. Without the mix of tough love and unconditional support, I would not have made it this far in life, and for that, I am forever grateful.

The last two people I want to thank are my kids. I wrote this book because of the experiences we have shared together on and off the playing field. You have provided me with a life I never knew existed. I know I can be intense from time to time. I know I can push you both hard from time to time. I honestly learn from you both more than you realize. You challenge me to be the best version of myself I possibly can. You inspire me daily. I am so grateful to be a part of your life and be able to love you forever and ever. I wish you would both slow down growing and getting older, because I am just having so much fun at this point in life, raising you both and doing all the cool and fun things that we do as a family. I hope this never changes and that we will always be close.

ABOUT THE AUTHOR

Cody Seevers is a decorated military officer, small business owner, coach, and now author. Raised in Ramona, CA, he was a competitive athlete in wrestling, football, and motocross, developing the resilience and discipline that would later define his career.

In 2009, Cody joined the U.S. Coast Guard, serving 10 years as an enlisted Operations Specialist before earning his commission through Officer Candidate School in 2020. Over his career, he has received three Coast Guard Commendation Medals, a Coast Guard Achievement Medal, and several other service awards. He holds a Bachelor of Science degree in Homeland Security and Public Safety.

Cody has been married to his wife, Blake, for 16 years, and together they are raising their two amazing children, Aislynn and Ezra, in Cape Cod, MA. Passionate about shaping young athletes, he coaches various sports teams his kids are involved in, witnessing firsthand both the rewards and the challenges of youth sports.

His book, Youth Sports Are Killing Me Slowly, was born out of frustration. Searching for guidance in the chaos of youth sports, he found no satisfying answers—so he wrote the book himself. His mission is to expose the flaws in the system and advocate for a healthier, more balanced approach to youth athletics.

Cody lives by the mantra: The culture you surround yourself with is the culture you will become. Through his leadership, coaching, and writing, he strives to create a positive impact on the next generation of athletes.

www.ingramcontent.com/pod-product-compliance
Lightning Source LLC
LaVergne TN
LVHW030630080426
835512LV00021B/3444